Conwy Castle
and Town Walls

Arnold Taylor CBE, DLitt, FBA

'Princely and Plesant'

'In my Lord Cliffordes return from Ireland, his Lordship landed nere your castle in Wales. For the maner of building it, scituacion, and prospectes about it, he sayes he never sawe any more princely and plesant but Winsor Castle. His Lordship would fayne have gone into the castle, but it is so ruinous that he could not do it without danger. He laments much the ruens of it, and says he is very sory he shall not be at London this winter, that he might perswade your lordship to repayr it. A small charg will yet kepe it up and make it habytable, which, if it stay a litell longer without it, a greadele will not do it ...'

Letter from Frances, Lady Pelham, to her brother, Edward, 2nd Viscount Conway and Killultagh (7 November 1635).

Every year visitors in their thousands walk through the empty ruins of Conwy Castle. As they climb to its battlements and look down through the floorless towers and roofless rooms, all of them, young and old alike, ponder on its meaning and its story. When and how was it built? Why was it built where it is? Why, indeed, was it built at all? What did it look like in its prime? What were all its different towers and rooms used for? What part has it played in history? How did it come to be ruined? And what of the town walls? Have they any special interest? It is the purpose of this guide to try to answer these and other questions to which a visit to the castle or a walk round the walled town gives rise.

The story of Conwy as we know it today, a picturesque walled town dominated by the turrets and battlements of its famous castle, begins in 1283. In that year the English armies of King Edward I (1272–1307) completed the conquest of Snowdonia and terminated the rule of the Welsh princes. In its place the Statute of Wales, issued by the king from Rhuddlan Castle a year later, inaugurated a new order based on a division of the principality into shires on the English pattern, with the northern shires (Anglesey, Caernarvonshire and Merioneth) looking to Caernarfon as their capital. We know, however, from a preliminary draft of the Statute,

that it was at first proposed to centre one of the counties — that which in the event became Caernarvonshire — not on Caernarfon but on Conwy. It seems probable, therefore, that at the time the building of the castle and borough was first decided on, it was primarily with the idea of establishing Conwy as the shire town. Though it did not, as things turned out, achieve this status, it was nevertheless, from its foundation, the largest of the north Wales boroughs.

King Edward I established the castle and borough at Conwy in 1283. He is seen here in a marginal drawing from an exchequer roll from 1300–01 (Public Record Office, E 368/72).

Opposite: Seen from almost any direction, the most striking feature of Conwy Castle is perhaps the unity and compactness of its design. This view from the east, with Thomas Telford's suspension bridge in the foreground, shows the Chapel Tower and King's Tower looming over the east barbican.

sic collato: memoria donatoris indelebi
liter perpetuetur. Et hoc tali largitate op

A History of Conwy Castle

Building the Town and Castle: 1283–92

The capture on 18 January 1283 of the native Welsh stronghold of Dolwyddelan gave the English command of the Conwy valley. Edward I himself moved up to Conwy from Rhuddlan on or about 14 March, and within four days of his arrival there arrangements were being made to secure labour for work on the new fortifications. Before the end of the month we find the master engineer, Richard of Chester, being sent from Conwy to Chester to commandeer tools and equipment for digging the rock-cut ditches and to recruit masons and stone-cutters. The king remained at Conwy until the beginning of May, by which time we may suppose the decisions had been taken which settled the siting and plan of both halves of the new works. The castle and walled town were complementary and their building proceeded simultaneously from the first. Their establishment involved the uprooting and removal to a new site at Maenan, 8 miles (13km) further up the river, of the abbey of Aberconwy, the principal Cistercian house of north Wales and burial place of Llywelyn the Great (d. 1240). The unfinished abbey church was retained and adapted to serve as the parish church of the new town, which it still remains.

The design and direction of the works was in the hands of James of St George, the greatest military architect of the age. Before entering the English royal service to become Master of the King's Works in Wales, St George had served as household architect to the king's cousin, Count Philip of Savoy (d. 1285), from whose castle of St Georges d'Espéranche, near Lyons, he took his name. Closely associated with him at Conwy was Richard of Chester, mentioned above, Master Henry of Oxford and Master Laurence of Canterbury, the principal master carpenters, and

John Francis, a mason probably brought by Master James from Savoy. They had charge over a force of craftsmen and labourers drawn from every corner of England and calculated to have numbered, when the work was at its height in the summer of 1285, something like 1,500 strong. At Saillon, in Switzerland (canton Valais), we can still see a well-documented example of a little castle and walled town which John Francis contracted to build for Count Peter of Savoy (d. 1268) in 1262, and which has marked resemblances to the style and workmanship typical of Conwy twenty years later (p. 39).

The cost in the money of the time, so far as can be ascertained from the figures that have come

Above: The reverse of the great seal of King Edward I (Public Record Office).

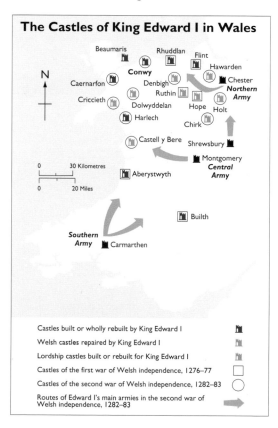

The Castles of King Edward I in Wales

N

Beaumaris
Rhuddlan
Flint
Hawarden
Conwy
Caernarfon
Denbigh
Chester
Northern Army
Criccieth
Ruthin
Dolwyddelan
Hope
Holt
Harlech
Chirk
Castell y Bere
Shrewsbury
Montgomery
Central Army
0   30 Kilometres
0   20 Miles
Aberystwyth
Builth
Southern Army
Carmarthen

Castles built or wholly rebuilt by King Edward I
Welsh castles repaired by King Edward I
Lordship castles built or rebuilt for King Edward I
Castles of the first war of Welsh independence, 1276–77
Castles of the second war of Welsh independence, 1282–83
Routes of Edward I's main armies in the second war of Welsh independence, 1282–83

Opposite: In this mid-thirteenth century manuscript illustration, a king is seen directing his master mason with construction work underway in the background (By permission of the British Library, Cotton Nero Ms. D I, f. 23v).

A reconstruction of Conwy Castle as it may have appeared towards the end of the thirteenth century. The turrets surrounding the inner ward with its royal apartments can be seen to the left, and the outer ward with the bow-shaped great hall range to the right (Illustration by Terry Ball, 1997).

down to us, cannot have been far short of £15,000. Though the accounts for the works extend over the period March 1283 to September 1292, the great bulk of the expenditure was incurred in a period of only four and a half years, and the whole structure we see today, begun in the spring of 1283, must have been substantially complete by the autumn of 1287. The fortress conceived and created in those few summers remains one of the outstanding achievements of medieval military architecture.

Repair and Maintenance: 1321–1627

Stonework, if well built and not deliberately pulled down, endures. Woodwork on the other hand, if not constantly protected from wind and weather,

deteriorates comparatively quickly. Leaky roofs and blocked gutters, leading to the rotting and eventual collapse of main timbers, are not new problems. At Conwy they had asserted themselves within a generation of the castle's completion, and, as the records from the fourteenth to the seventeenth century show, their recurrence was perennial. In this Conwy was not exceptional. From the first, the structural maintenance of the north Wales castles showed scant respect for the genius of their creators.

As originally finished, the internal buildings of the castle, and in all probability the eight towers as well, were roofed with shingles or slates. Without constant repair such roofs could not stand up to the prevailing climate. Consequently, as early as 1321, we read that 'in the Hall of Conwy Castle several of the roof trusses have failed, and in other buildings and towers many of the trusses and much of the rest of the timber have perished for want of a covering of lead'.

Estimates were given but little appears to have been done: in 1332 it was reported of Conwy and the other castles that 'the king understands they are ruinous and not fit for him to dwell in if he should go there'.

In 1343, a detailed survey of Conwy was carried out just after the grant of his Welsh inheritance to Edward, the Black Prince (d. 1376). It disclosed that in six out of the eight towers, as well as in many of the courtyard buildings, the roofs were unsafe because of old and rotting timber, resulting from the lack of lead roofs. At least three years later, major works of reconstruction were undertaken under the direction of the prince's mason, Henry de Snelleston. Lead roofs were substituted throughout the castle, and in order to bear their weight (with that of the earth or clay that it was customary to lay between the lead and the wood) fifteen great stone arches, of which only two now survive, were substituted for the original wooden trusses in the great hall range and royal apartments (pp. 20–21 and 28–31). Some or all of the tower roofs may have been reconstructed at this time also. At wall-top level one may still see extensive evidence of how the new leadwork was 'flashed' or edged into the base of the battlements (p. 37); when the lead roofing was wrenched from the masonry in the course of the dismantling of the castle in 1665, the grooving we see today was exposed.

These works, begun in the year of the battle of Crécy (1346), were the only major modifications made to the castle buildings throughout their history. The claims of minor maintenance must, however, have been ever present, and some of the responses to them, as likewise the small alterations effected at different periods to meet changing occupational requirements, are mentioned below in describing the various individual buildings. The impression left by the records is one of long periods of neglect, interspersed with periodic attempts to arrest decay, the latter sometimes to make a show for a special occasion as, for instance, the 'reparacions done upon the Castell of Conwey by Hugh Peicke agaynst the comyng of the lorde Precedent and other the Kynges most honourable Counseill of the Marches into North Wales' in 1541. Even in those days ivy was a menace to be reckoned with, and in 1537 we read, amongst payments for cleansing the gutters, of 1/2d. 'payed for pyche to bryn an evyeroote ther' and 4d. 'payd to Hugh

Tona to make fyer to the same roote'. The root must have been a specially noxious specimen, for it was the custom at this time to lay out 2s. 0d. in any case 'for clansyng and cuttyng evyns upon the ledys of the Castell for the hole yer'.

The battle of the roofs was a losing one, and in the changed conditions resulting after 1485 from the accession of a Welsh dynasty to the English throne, there must have seemed less and

Left: In May 1343, Edward, prince of Wales (1343–76), 'the Black Prince', inherited the Crown lands in the principality. A survey of Conwy made for the prince in that year disclosed serious problems with the castle roofs. Modifications were undertaken in 1346–47, including the insertion of a total of fifteen great stone arches in the great hall range and the royal apartments of the inner ward. The repairs were the work of the prince's master mason, Henry de Snelleston. This watercolour by Thomas Girtin (1775–1802) shows the two surviving arches in the hall range; one of these has since collapsed (© Copyright British Museum).

Below: The gilt-bronze effigy of Edward, the Black Prince, rests in Canterbury Cathedral.

Conwy, about 1600

Produced by an unknown artist about 1600, this magnificent drawing presents an early 'bird's-eye view' of Conwy. The castle and the garden in its east barbican appear in the foreground, with the town surrounded by its walls in the distance. St Mary's church is depicted clearly at the centre of the town, and above this the large house is Plas Mawr, built 1576–85 (By permission of the marquess of Salisbury, Hatfield House, CPM 1/62).

less need to wage it. Consequently it is not surprising to learn, from a detailed survey made in 1627, that the whole building was then in decline and dangerous to enter, 'the leads being decayed and broken above and almost all the floares fallen downe'. In that year the castle was accordingly sold for £100 by the Commissioners for the sale of the king's lands to one of the leading political figures of the day. This was Charles I's Secretary of State, Edward, Lord Conway of Ragley, Warwickshire, a Welshman and cousin to Sir John Conway of Bodrhyddan. Recently created Viscount Conway of Killultagh, County Antrim, he promptly marked his new acquisition by assuming the title of Viscount Conway of Conway Castle, and was thenceforward known as Lord Conway and Killultagh.

The Castle and the Civil War

The first Lord Conway died in 1631, and for a time there was a possibility that his son would repair the castle and make it his principal seat. Towards the end of 1635 he wrote to his cousin at Bodrhyddan saying how glad he was to hear that the walls were still so good and asking Sir John's assistance in procuring additional land in the district and discovering what privileges were attached to the tenure of the castle. He had heard there was plenty of lead, and he said that when he should be able to repair the buildings he would obtain whatever new timber was necessary from his estates in Ireland. But the times were out of joint, and, as the mounting conflict between king and parliament hardened into civil war, the castle's chances of becoming a nobleman's residence passed for ever. It was soon to be put in order, for the last time, to serve sterner needs.

It so happened that one of King Charles's chief adherents at this juncture, the celebrated John Williams (1582–1650), successively dean of Westminster, bishop of Lincoln and archbishop of York, was a Conwy-born man. Williams was much alive to the potentialities of Conwy in a struggle now being waged by force of arms, and took it on himself to garrison and fortify the castle and make it a rallying point for the Royalist gentry of the neighbourhood. Having done so, early in 1645 he demanded to be given the governorship

Top: A survey of the castle made in 1627 provides a room-by-room description. It is clear from the survey that the whole structure was in a dangerous state 'with the leads being decayed and broken above and almost all the floares fallen downe' (Public Record Office, SP 16/89/25).

Above left: Only a few months after the survey, the castle was bought by Lord Conway of Ragley (1563–1631), Secretary of State to King Charles I (1625–49). He promptly assumed the title of Viscount Conway of Conway Castle. Lord Conway is seen here in a detail from an engraving of 1624 entitled 'Great Brittaines Noble and worthy Councell of Warr' (By courtesy of the National Portrait Gallery, London).

Left: John Williams (1582–1650), exiled archbishop of York, returned to his native Conwy to defend it for King Charles I during the Civil War of the 1640s. This engraving depicts the archbishop exchanging his mitre for a helmet (Ashmolean Museum, Oxford).

The Castle Building Materials

Visitors may wonder how, over 700 years ago, materials could be obtained for great enterprises like the Conwy buildings, where they could come from and how they could be brought to the site. Such contemporary building accounts as survive supply us with part of the answer, while a good deal can be learned from the enduring materials of which the ruins themselves are composed.

Among the latter, three different kinds of building stone are identifiable. By far the greater proportion of castle and town walls alike is built of the hard grey Silurian grit of which the castle rock itself is formed; probably it was obtained near at hand, and the very large quarry on the Llangelynin road, not far outside the Upper Gate, may have been one of the principal sources.

Secondly, in the northern and eastern parts of the town walls and in the spur wall, considerable

quantities of rhyolite are used; this yellowish-brown rock could have been obtained very near at hand, for Bodlondeb Hill and Conwy Mountain are both formed of it.

Finally, nearly all the freestone used in features such as arrowloops, windows, door jambs, and chimney-pieces, both in the castle and on the walls, is a pinkish sandstone probably obtained from the Creuddyn peninsula on the opposite side of the river. On the other hand, the sandstone used for the fourteenth-century roof-arches is known to have been shipped to Conwy from the neighbourhood of Chester.

Water transport played a big part in the building of this as of all the north Wales coastal castles. Timber, of which very large quantities were required, was brought down the river from Trefriw and beyond. Lead, and coal for the forges of the smiths, came by sea from near Flint. Iron and steel and nails were purchased at Newcastle-under-Lyme, brought overland to Chester and thence by water. Sand for making the mortar was brought across the river from Deganwy. Purple slate, used here and there for bedding and levelling courses in the thirteenth-century work, and perhaps also for much of the original roofing, may have come, as it did in the sixteenth century, by boat from Ogwen or by cart from Llangelynin, 3 miles (5km) away. Special items, like the image for the castle chapel, were bought in Chester. Simon the Glazier of Chester, who supplied glass to Caernarfon in 1283, probably did the same for Conwy.

in place of Sir John Owen of Clenenney, whom he disliked and despised; '*from the bare walls*', he wrote, '*I have repaired, victualled, and supplied it with ammunition at mine own charges, and I am more likely to give his Majesty a good account for it than this gentleman is, who without my costs and charges was never able to repair the town as now it is, nor hath he any arms but what I lent him to defend it*'. We know from another record that, in order to furnish the castle, Williams borrowed hangings and other articles from local sympathizers.

Having backed the losing side with all his resources, and receiving no thanks for doing so, the archbishop threw in his lot with the enemy. In the end, Williams assisted the parliamentary Major-General Thomas Mytton (d. 1656), whose forces were besieging Conwy, so as to save his native town from destruction. In November 1646 the castle surrendered. For the next five years, Colonel John Carter, the governor appointed by parliament, kept it on a war footing. The following extracts from his expenses are worthy of record:

For new laying and repairing Platformes for the great Guns in the Castle, as also for mounting and fitting those Guns, with springes, ladles, and Ironworke, and repaireing their Carriages at severall times £10 12s. 0d.

Paid for altering and repaireing 3 draw Bridges belonging the said Garrison that were shattered and spoyled in the time of the siege, and for making a new Gate and Turnepike for the necessary safety of the Garrison £12 6s. 0d.

Paid for new leadding of a Top Tower in Conwy Castle, and for repaireing the Leades and windowes of the Castle £16 0s. 0d.

For Iron bars for windows and other ironwork for safe keeping of prisoners £1 16s. 0d.

In 1655 the Council of State ordered the fortifications in Conwy and Caernarfon to be slighted, so as to render the castles untenable. At Conwy, this is the most likely explanation of the massive breach long to be seen in the outward wall of the Bakehouse Tower, causing it to be known as the *twr darn* or 'broken tower' until its major repair by the railway company in the nineteenth century. Effected at a point where it would weaken the defence of both the outer and inner wards of the castle, the position for the breach could not

have been better chosen. Moreover, the scale of the damage to near-impregnable masonry points to gunpowder as the only possible agent of destruction, as at so many other castles. The long-accepted story that it resulted from digging for stone by the avaricious inhabitants has always seemed unconvincing.

Dismantling and Abandonment: 1665

At the Restoration of Charles II in 1660 the castle was returned to the third Lord Conway. Like a hundred others, it had been left by the fortunes of war a building beyond economic repair. One can hardly blame its owner for deciding to sell what little was saleable and abandon the rest. In fact, all that was worth selling was the lead and the timber, and in 1665 Lord Conway sent his agent Williams Milward from Ragley to supervise the dismantling, and arrange for the sale of the lead. We have a series of letters in which, writing back from Conwy, Milward tells his master in vivid detail of the obstacles put in his way by the local worthies, who were suspicious of his credentials and who, as he said, 'were misgreeved att the taking of it downe'. He secured the help of '*a verye knowing man from Blew Morris [Beaumaris] which doth most of the best worke in Anglelsea, and hath*

Major-General Thomas Mytton (d. 1656) from John Vicars's England's Worthies... *(London 1647). Mytton commanded the parliamentary forces that besieged Conwy Castle in 1646 (By permission of the British Library).*

The lead from the castle roofs and wall tops was one of the most valuable materials to be salvaged from the castle in the 1660s. A narrow 'creasing' marks the position where the lead was originally bedded into the masonry at wall-walk level.

Joseph Mallord William Turner (1775–1851) probably completed this majestic oil painting of Conwy in 1802–03; it was based on the artist's tours in north Wales in 1798–99. Turner sought to capture the 'sublime' and overwhelming emotions felt by many late eighteenth- and early nineteenth-century travellers in the mountainous landscapes of Wales (By kind permission of his grace the duke of Westminster TD, DL).

hopen to take downe a Castell or two alredye'.

Even so the task was not a simple one. The timber was so rotten that taking it to pieces was dangerous to life and limb, and when it was down it was not to be easily disposed of: *'the farmers of the countrye and the meaner sort would buy, but they have no money, and the rich will not buy unlese they have a bargaine'.* The lead, on the other hand, was so valuable as to be under constant threat of theft, and Milward had to resort to an early experiment in flood-lighting to foil the pilferers: *'I have secured all places where I can judge to be any danger, and some nights have had men there great part of the night, and set up great lights that the cuntrye might take notice that there was men lay in the castell'.* Well might he add, *'My Lord, I have found a verye troublesome and dangerous peece of worke in takeing upp of this lead, which I did somewhat foresee before I*

came, and I find it proves according to my expectation'. But in due course the sorry work was finished, and the main structure of the castle thereafter consigned to withstand the assaults of time and nature as best it might.

The Nineteenth and Twentieth Centuries

The opening of Thomas Telford's road bridge in 1826, and the building of the tubular bridge and opening of the Chester and Holyhead Railway in 1848, both served to bring Conwy's remarkable monuments to wider notice and so to lead indirectly to moves to secure their better preservation. One of the earliest of these emanated from the university of

Oxford and resulted, in 1876, in an agreement by which the keeper of the Ashmolean Museum, John Henry Parker (1806–84), with the consent of the town of Conwy, 'restored at his own cost and expense the floors of the high tower in the medieval walls of the said town with a view to the preservation thereof ... as also to keep and maintain the said high tower clean and in a fit state for visitors who may wish to inspect the same and to sit there or to sketch therein or therefrom'.

It was about this time, too, that the London and North Western Railway Company undertook the rebuilding of the 'broken tower' of the castle (see p. 34), together with a number of minor repairs on the railway side of the town walls. By the end of the century the walls, as well as the castle, were beginning to be seen to have an interest of their own, and in 1898 the wall-walk between the spur wall and the Upper Gate was opened to visitors, concrete footbridges being provided across the open gorges of Towers 5 to 9 and 11 to 14.

Meanwhile there had been an important change in another direction. For many years the Conways' successors, the Seymours, marquesses of Hertford, had leased their Conwy properties to a well-known local family, the Hollands. In 1865 the representatives of the Hollands, with the assent of the fourth marquess of Hertford, assigned their rights in the castle to the mayor, bailiffs and free burgesses of Conwy, so that in effect it passed into the possession of the town. A further change came about in 1885 when, on the death of Sir Richard Bulkeley, the last constable appointed directly by the Crown, Queen Victoria issued Letters Patent granting to the mayor of the town for the time being the office of constable of the castle, 'with all liberties, privileges and advantages to the said office belonging'. It was thus that responsibility for the upkeep of the castle came to be wholly vested in the local authority, who continued to discharge it until 1953.

In that year the Corporation entered into an agreement with the Ministry of Works, whereby the care and administration of the castle and town walls were transferred to the Ministry for a period of ninety-nine years. Since then a comprehensive programme of repair and conservation of the whole monument has been steadily proceeding under the Ministry and its

Above: A photograph of about 1868–70, in which carriages are seen below the outer gate, their drivers doubtless awaiting visitors viewing the castle ruins.

Left: Since 1953, the care and administration of the castle and town walls have been the responsibility of the State. This 1955 view of the great hall range shows conservation underway by the Ministry of Works, a predecessor of Cadw.

successors. It is now maintained by Cadw, on behalf of the National Assembly for Wales.

In 1987, Conwy Castle and town walls, together with Beaumaris, Harlech, and Caernarfon, were inscribed on the World Heritage List as a historic site of outstanding universal value.

A Tour of Conwy Castle

The Castle Plan

Anyone looking at Conwy Castle for the first time will be impressed first and foremost by the unity and compactness of so great a mass of building, with its eight almost identical towers, four on the north and four on the south, pinning it to the rock on which it stands. Especially striking is the long northern front, where the towers' equidistant spacing divides the wall surface into three exactly similar sections, each pierced by a similar pair of arrowloops, and each rising to a common battlement line. Closer inspection, however, shows that the four eastern towers are distinguished from the others by the addition of surmounting turrets, and this superficial variation in their treatment is of more than merely architectural significance. It reflects a fundamental division within; the accommodation the castle was built to provide being in fact planned in two quite separate halves, each with its own ward or courtyard and each with its independent way of entry from the outside world (see plan inside the back cover).

The inner ward, towards the east, could be directly approached only by water (pp. 35–36), an arrangement affording the utmost security for the sovereign personage for whose lodging it was devised. It is round this ward that the four turreted towers are grouped, and they were doubtless so designed that they might fly the king's standards from their tops when the court should be at Conwy and provide high look-out points for watchmen guarding the four corners of a royal residence. The larger outer ward, towards the west, was approached from within the town, and to that extent was the less isolated part of the building. It accommodated the permanent garrison of the castle. This followed a fixed establishment, laid down in 1284. First, with his family and his household,

was the constable, a royal nominee directly responsible to the king for the safe-keeping of the castle, of state prisoners entrusted to his custody, and of the town of which he was *ex officio* mayor. Under him and maintained at his cost (his annual stipend even in 1284 was £190) was a body of thirty fencible men, of whom fifteen were crossbowmen and the rest were porters, watchmen and other castle servants; there were also a resident chaplain, a mason, a carpenter, a smith and an armourer. It is probable that the constable and his family occupied the two westernmost towers, commanding the principal gate, and that the rooms in the other two outer ward towers were assigned as lodgings and offices for the other permanent officials.

A view along the northern side of the castle, showing numerous arrowloops in the walls, towers and battlements. Traces of the white limewash that originally covered the entire castle can also be seen.

Opposite: An aerial view of the castle and the town walls seen from the south-east. The defences were regarded as a single entity, with entrance to the castle's outer gate gained from within the fortified town.

The north-west tower and the outer gate display many of the characteristic features to be seen in the external walls of the castle. The numbers highlight several of those features described in the text.

External Features

Some of the most interesting points about the castle are to be seen from the outside. We know that when the walls and towers were first completed they were limewashed, and the whiteness of the building, with the town at its foot and only the green hills and river around it, must have made it a striking landmark. Traces of the whitening can still be seen in many places [1], particularly on the southern towers (towards the railway) and on the curtain wall near the present approach path. Its presence on the turret of the east barbican nearest the Chapel Tower, seen from

the road below, is the only surviving indication of the line of the destroyed watergate approach as it curved round and up into this end of the castle (p. 36).

Another feature, puzzling at first, is the occurrence on the face of walls and towers alike of a line of small round holes spaced about 6 to 10 feet (1.8 to 3m) apart and set on a slant [2]. These are putlog holes, and their arrangement in this manner shows that the north Wales castle-builders (the same thing is conspicuous at Harlech and Beaumaris) followed the common French practice of using inclined, instead of horizontal, scaffolds, up which the heavy loads of stone could be wheeled or dragged as the building gradually rose higher. On the towers these holes often show as a regular helicoidal line spiralling round the exterior face of the masonry.

The round putlog holes, set thus on sloping alignments, are to be distinguished from the rather larger square holes which occur throughout the castle at a uniform level just below the battlements [3]. The purpose of these was to carry bearers for hourds, or projecting timber encasements, which could be extended at need in front of any part of the wall tops in time of siege. Another point of interest is the arrangement of the loops in the battlements themselves, so that they are always at alternating levels [4]. The practice is uniform throughout the castle and town walls, and appears to be designed to afford alternative fields of fire over the immediate or remoter foreground.

A castle like Conwy was by no means lacking in sanitation, and the latrines serving the rooms in the different towers are prominent on both sides of the building. On the south, towards the Gyffin stream, they take the form of corbelled projections overhanging the rock, and the remains of four such can be seen, one beside each tower. On the north, or entrance side, they are contained wholly or partly in thickened sections of the curtain wall, and here the chutes are visible at ground level. The shafts were large, and all four of these northern chutes were originally walled round as a protection against the risk of an intruder using them to gain entry to the castle. The arrangement is well seen against the north-west tower, where the little curved protecting wall is still intact.

Any window-opening wide enough to have been climbed through was originally heavily barred with an iron grille. The holes from which these grilles were

Left: The castle featured prominently in the events leading to the abdication of Richard II (1377–99) in 1399. This fifteenth-century manuscript illustration depicts John de Montague (d. 1400), earl of Salisbury and a loyal supporter of the king, landing at Conwy. The illustration conveys an impression of the white-rendered walls of the medieval fortress (By permission of the British Library, Harley Ms. 1319, f. 14v).

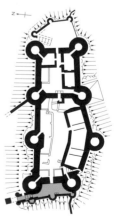

The south side of the castle overlooks the Gyffin stream. Here, the privies serving the rooms in the towers took the form of corbelled-out projections overhanging the rock. This one lies next to the Prison Tower.

wrenched when the castle was dismantled in the seventeenth century can still be seen round every window and loop of any size [5]. All the larger windows in the towers were of two lights, closed by shutters, but in many the centre mullion has perished. It will be noticed that these wider openings occur only at heights beyond the reach of scaling ladders.

Two other external characteristics, one of the castle as it is, the other as it was, are notable. The first is the fact that outwardly the towers are not truly perpendicular but are very slightly sloped or 'battered', tapering gradually and with such skilful masoncraft that, where the slope finally dies into the straight, the change is almost imperceptible. The second is the way in which the battlements were decorated with little finials or pinnacles [6]. A few of these remain; but originally there were two or three to every merlon, and, as some of the eighteenth-century prints show, they must have added a pleasing touch of lightness to the sombre strengths below.

The castle has been roofless for more than three hundred years and there is now no conclusive evidence of the original form and shape of the roofs of the towers. It is clear that most of the tower roofs

underwent radical reconstruction in the medieval period, and there is some reference to tower roofs being renewed in the accounts of Henry VIII's time. An original inner ring of masonry which survives on the south-west tower may have circled the base of a conical roof which would, perhaps, have risen a little higher than the tops of the battlements. This may well have been the form of all the tower roofs at first.

In short, therefore, one may visualize a castle that had white walls, barred and shuttered windows, and the tops of conical roofs peeping up from behind the pinnacled battlements of its towers (see page 6).

The Outer Gate and West Barbican

The original approach to the castle from within the walled town took the form of a long, stepped ramp. Constructed of solid masonry, this led straight up from road level to a point at which it was separated from the castle by an artificial chasm bridged only by a drawbridge. As long ago as 1627, surveyors

reported of this latter that there remained '*nothing but some rotten beames, all the Planks beinge gone, and noe meanes to goe over but with dainger*'.
A sloping path now winds up the castle rock across the bridge from the visitor centre, and at the top we are brought into the passage of the outer gatehouse through a modern opening forced in its side wall.

The gateway from the west barbican into the outer ward was defended by an elaborate series of machicolations, or 'murder holes'.

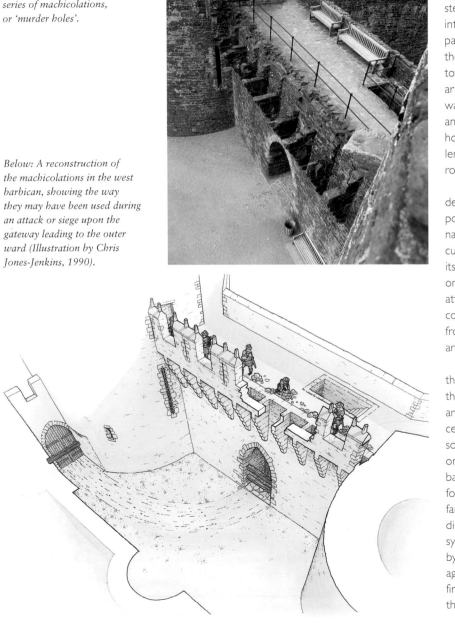

Below: A reconstruction of the machicolations in the west barbican, showing the way they may have been used during an attack or siege upon the gateway leading to the outer ward (Illustration by Chris Jones-Jenkins, 1990).

Recessed into the thickness of the opposite wall are the remains of narrow steps which led to an upper level whence the working of the drawbridge and portcullis (the grooves for which are seen just behind the entrance arch on the right) was controlled. The pivot holes for the axle of the drawbridge, and what is left of the former ramped approach from street level, can be seen from a modern look-out platform erected within the lower part of the original gate-passage. From this platform a flight of modern steps, steeper than the old ascent, leads on up into the west barbican, the upper end of the passage being marked by an arch, of which only the springers remain, between the great north-west tower and the adjacent turret, in which a short arrowloop covers the top of the stairs. The arch was closed by two-leaved doors, opening inwards, and now evidenced by their hinge and drawbar holes. Though now open to the sky, the whole length of the outer gate-passage was originally roofed over.

The west barbican is a small outer enclosure designed to screen and protect what was always potentially the most vulnerable point of the defences, namely, the wide gate leading through the main curtain wall into the interior of the castle. While its primary purpose was to impede direct attack on the gate, it would also effectively contain any attackers who might have reached thus far in a confined space where they could be dealt with from the wall tops and the flanking towers. Its arrangements are simple and practical.

On the right are three open turrets, low on the inside, but on the outside, rising sheer from the rocks of the western ditch, whose depths their arrowloops could sweep with fire. On the left, centred between the massive north-west and south-west towers, is the vital gateway, commanded on either side by great arrowloops, originally heavily barred, and elevated so as to overlook the whole foreground of the entrance. Above, projecting far out from the curtain itself along the whole distance from tower to tower, is an elaborate system of 'machicolations', originally surmounted by a battlemented parapet of which only the ends against the towers remain. Its presence added the final touch to the hazards of any attempt to attack the wall, or to burn or batter down the gate.

The Outer Ward

The outer ward, which we now enter from the west barbican, occupies rather more than two-thirds of the main castle area. On the north, east and west it is straight-sided, but on the south it is bowed outwards to allow the buildings within it to occupy the full extent of the promontory on which the castle stands. Originally, there were buildings against all four curtain walls, leaving a much smaller open area than we see today. On the west was a range containing guardrooms or porters' lodges, on the north a kitchen and a stable, on the east the gatehouse to the inner ward (with an adjacent wellhouse) and on the south the rooms that comprised the long curving range of the great hall. Those on the east and south remain standing. A wide pitched-stone path, curving to follow the line of the hall range, runs the full length of the ward. A small stone foundation beside it is thought to have been part of the base of a leaden conduit or water tank. The ward is flanked by six towers, one at each corner and one half-way along each of the longer sides. The two eastern towers are common to both wards but will be described with the buildings of the inner ward from which they are entered.

The Main Gate and Guardrooms

The gate comprised a threefold barrier. First, there were two heavy drawbars, sliding in holes still visible on either side of the entry; next, there was a portcullis; and lastly, two-leaved wooden doors of which the hinge and drawbar holes can also be seen. High up on the south side there is a flight of steps in the thickness of the wall. These led down from the wall-walk to a small chamber from which the portcullis was worked: it occupied the upper part of

A view of the outer ward looking west, with the bow-shaped great hall range to the left. In the foreground, the Stockhouse and Bakehouse Towers stand at either end of the wall which separates the largely administrative outer ward from the royal apartments of the inner ward.

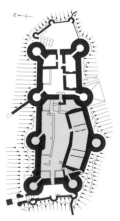

the lofty gate arch and also connected with the first floor of the short range of buildings formerly backing on the gate. Of these buildings only the footings now remain. A survey made in 1627 says that it contained '*a low darke roome*' on either side of the gate-passage, with '*twoe stories of roomes*' extending over them; '*the Walls*', it continues, '*are all fallen downe towards the Court, but the twoe ends and the Castle wall keepe up the Coveringe which is lead, a little broken in some places, but not much decayed*'. The building is presumably that mentioned as the '*porters logge*' in an account of 1531, its upper floors then consisting of the '*porters chamber*' and a '*loft*'. The corbels that supported its roof still project from the wall above the gate.

An impression of the eastern half of the great hall range as it may have appeared in the late 1280s. The hall itself appears in the foreground, with the timber-framed partitions partly removed to reveal the chapel beyond (Illustration by Terry Ball, 1998).

The Kitchen and Stable

These buildings have likewise been destroyed to the ground, but their footings have been exposed and preserved. Practically all we know about them is derived from the 1627 survey. From this it appears that the kitchen occupied approximately the western three-quarters of the range and the stable the remaining quarter at the east end, the division probably coming where there is the foundation of a respond, or return wall, opposite the embrasure nearest the door of the Kitchen Tower. In 1627 the walls of the building still stood, '*but the roofe is fallen downe, and lead and timber lies all togeather on the ground*'. The smaller room, which the surveyors took to be a stable '*by an old Manger that still continues there*', was in the same condition. A survey taken in 1343 described the kitchen, brewhouse and bakehouse as all being placed under one roof, which explains the length of the kitchen building; at that time they were already in bad disrepair.

The Great Hall Range

The 'great hall' is the name traditionally used to cover the whole length of the long curving range that occupies the greater part of the south side of the outer ward. Its interior was formerly divided into separate sections by timber-framed partitions, the exact position of which can now only be conjectured. To the left (east) of the entrance doorway from the courtyard was the castle chapel, its altar occupying the recess below the great round-headed east window, and with light also coming from two windows on the south and one of the three large traceried windows towards the courtyard. The entrance door, originally covered by a porch, probably opened into a broad passage separating the chapel from three interconnecting rooms on the right (west), their number and arrangement being reflected today in the positions of their three fireplaces. The largest room, opening directly from the passage and having the largest of the three fireplaces, would have been the hall proper, lit principally by the middle of the three two-light windows facing the courtyard; from the embrasure of a smaller window on the south side there is direct

access to the stair of the Prison Tower, and so via the wall-walk to all parts of the castle. The remainder of the range, judging from the position of the fireplaces in the northern and western walls, could have been used to provide two withdrawing rooms.

The roof of the range was of nine bays, and was supported on eight great stone arches. Four of these had fallen away by 1835, and now only one survives. Nevertheless, parts of the springers of most of the others, or at least the seatings from which they have been torn, can still be seen. Careful scrutiny shows that the arches were not of one build with the walls, but were, in fact, later insertions into the fabric. This is because the stone-arched roof was a modification introduced in the time of the Black Prince. In 1346–47, the prince's mason, Henry de Snelleston, replaced the

original wooden-arched roof of 1284–86. Of this latter there are still many traces, especially a number of the broken stumps of the grey stone corbels which supported the feet of the trusses.

The floor of the hall range, which is now missing, was carried partly on the rock (where you are now standing) and partly, to the south, on heavy close-set timber joists. The bearer holes for these joists appear as a prominent feature all along the south wall. The space under this southern half of the range served as a long narrow cellar, reached by steps leading down from the courtyard to a passage under the west end. There was an inner cellar underneath the chapel at the east end of the range. A modern wooden bridge has been provided to give access to the Prison Tower.

The unusual bowed shape of the great hall range was determined by the nature of the castle site. Although it now appears as one long room, the interior was originally divided into separate parts by timber-framed partitions. The roof of the whole range was at first supported on timber trusses, though these were replaced in the 1340s by eight great stone arches. Only one of these arches now survives complete. The northern half of the range lies directly on the rock, while the floor to the south was of timber set over a narrow cellar.

The north-west and south-west towers at the entrance to the outer ward are to be regarded as parts of a single unit of accommodation, probably intended for the castle constable.

Built some five or six years earlier, the twin-towered west gatehouse at Rhuddlan provides a model for the arrangements to be seen at the entrance to the outer ward at Conwy.

The Towers of the Outer Ward

The North-West Tower

Having looked at the buildings within the four walls of the ward, we may now turn to its towers. All have lost their intermediate floors, but the two western towers, in which the newel staircases have been reconstructed, are fully accessible to visitors through to battlement level. The north-west tower, entered through a rebuilt doorway in the angle of the courtyard (that is, from within the site of the destroyed northern guardroom), contains a basement and two upper rooms. The basement has two loops to light it and was intended for storage, not incarceration. Each of the upper chambers has a fireplace and one main two-light window with window seats in the embrasures, as well as small windows, and both were therefore suitable for use as living-rooms or offices. Opening off the staircase half-way between them is a narrow passage leading through a small pentagonal mural chamber to a latrine.

The South-West Tower

The south-west tower is entered from a little enclosed yard at the west end of the great hall, reached up a short flight of steps from the courtyard. Its arrangements are closely similar to those just described, with the difference that here the basement room contains an oven. The upper rooms each have their fireplace and their large and small windows, while on this side both floors have their own latrine corbelled out above the rocks beside the Gyffin.

The north-west and south-west towers are to be regarded, with the curtain wall and porter's building which served to link them across the intervening gate-passage, as parts of a single unit, and there is little doubt that together they would have been occupied by the constable. In effect the whole block was the equivalent of the twin-towered gatehouses built five or six years earlier at Rhuddlan, the difference being that at Conwy the great flanking towers are set farther apart in order that the gate unit may be stretched to occupy the full extent of the castle rock. Even so they are still closer together than any other two towers in the castle, and, seen frontally from the west, plainly form a pair.

The Kitchen Tower

The Kitchen Tower is so named from its proximity to the kitchen from which it was entered. Like the towers previously described, it contained a basement intended for storage (possibly, in this case, as a larder) and two well-appointed upper rooms. The stairs have not been renewed, and the best view of the upper floors is therefore to be obtained from the landing at wall-walk level. The second-floor chimney-piece is particularly well preserved, and that of the room below it only a little less so.

The Prison Tower

The basement of this tower is differently arranged from those in the three towers described hitherto, and there can be no doubt that here was the real dungeon of the castle. Indeed it looks as if the very existence of the basement in this tower, which had four storeys as compared with the others' three, may have been intended to escape the observation of a casual searcher.

Entrance was by a narrow doorway inconspicuously placed in the side of one of the hall window embrasures, whence a short passage at the back of the central fireplace leads to the foot of the main tower staircase. From this point five steps lead down through two doors and a right-angled turn to a room which, when floored, must have looked in the prevailing semi-darkness very much like any of the three basement rooms already described.

The opening was about 4 feet (1.2m) above the floor — an easy jump for a habitué, a nasty drop for a stranger pushed from behind. The floor itself was supported on ten massive close-set beams, securely inserted in the walls during building; the holes in which they rested can be seen from above. A framing of this strength could have carried an earth or stone-flagged floor, conveying the illusion that it was the bottom of the tower. This, however, as we can now easily see, was not the case. For below the level of the beam holes the walls continue downwards in a circle of unrelieved smoothness, enclosing a pit whose only entry was through a trap, and whose only light and ventilation was a narrow shaft barely 18 inches (46cm) square in a wall 12 feet (3.7m) thick. This was indeed the point of no return.

The rooms above the two basements are similar to those in the other towers. Each has its fireplace and the usual assortment of large and small windows,

The Kitchen Tower was so named from its proximity to the kitchen, now represented by low foundations in the outer ward. In this illustration from the fourteenth-century Luttrell Psalter, a cook is shown preparing food in readiness for the great hall (By permission of the British Library, Additional Ms. 42130, f. 207v).

The inconspicuous narrow doorway, situated in the right-hand side of one of the great hall range window embrasures, leads into the Prison Tower.

A fifteenth-century manuscript illustration depicting an unfortunate prisoner in shackles. At Conwy, by the end of the Middle Ages, the upper basement in the Prison Tower was probably used to incarcerate debtors (By permission of the British Library, Harley Ms. 4375, f. 140).

In the maintenance accounts from the time of Henry VIII (1509–47), there are several references to the Prison Tower. This detail of the records for 1534 notes the payment for 'cleansing and carrying away the Mullok and erthe in the doungeon under the dettors Chambre' (Public Record Office, E 101/489/9).

while opening off the staircase at a mezzanine level is a latrine corbelled out over the rock in the angle between tower and curtain wall.

Maintenance accounts of the time of Henry VIII (1509–47) make several references to the Prison Tower, or, as it was then called, the Debtors Tower. In particular they show us that the upper basement was at that time in use as the 'Debtors Chamber'. In 1532 they record payments made to a mason 'for stoppyng the gret wyndoo with lyme and stone in the dettours chamber', and part of the blocking then inserted in the window-embrasure is still to be seen there. Other payments made at the same time are 'for boarding the said Dettours Chamber, 6d' and 'to laborers to clense the gret dongeon under the said chamber, 16d'. In 1534 there are payments for 'cleansing and carrying away the Mullok and erthe in the doungeon under the dettors Chambre', for 'making a door over the Dettours Chambre and mending the floor with boards', for 'a bedd Case for the Chambre over the dettours Chambre for prysoners' (2s. 4d.), and 'to the mason for settyng a hook in the wall in the same chamber'.

The Well and Middle Gate

The pitched-stone path through the centre of the outer ward terminates against a deep pit, the sides of which are walled in stone. This pit is the upper part of the castle well, and is formed in a wide cleft cut from north to south across the castle rock to isolate and strengthen the approach from the outer to the inner ward. The well is 91 feet (27.7m) deep and fed by a spring and the percolation of surface water. It was originally roofed as is shown by the conventional representation of a well-house in the drawing of about 1600. We read in accounts of 1525 of 5s. 0d. paid for 1,000 slates, with their carriage by boat from Ogwen, 'to sclate the oder side

[outside] of the well in the castell', and in 1531 of 'puttying of a new geiste [joist] over the well and makying a lydde to the same well'. The 1627 surveyors speak of it as 'a large drawe Well cutte downe into a Mayne rock; Water enough and singuler good'.

The western and northern sides of the well-pit are formed by a curving wall of solid masonry, 8 feet (2.4m) in thickness. To the east (as represented by the modern paved pathway), the curving wall was carried through from the well-pit to adjoin the masonry of the curtain between the two wards. At this point, it served to form the northern side of what was originally a deep V-shaped chasm (now marked by the area of gravel within the pathway). The chasm itself was spanned by a drawbridge, running parallel with the face of the curtain, and situated in front of the little projecting gatehouse covering the passage to the inner ward. This is the bridge referred to in a record of 1524, when one David ap Tudor was paid 2s. 4d. for working and making 'a newe brigge to entre into the ynder warde of the said Castell'. In 1531 we read again of repairs to the 'bridge next the ynder warde', but very shortly afterwards it must have been removed. In April 1532, one Roland Mason was paid for eight days' work 'makyng the wall about the well', that is the added wall which closes off the chasm under the site of the drawbridge and divides it from the well-pit. A few weeks later, on 6 and 7 May 1532, two labourers were engaged in 'fyllying with Robell & wrth [rubble and earth] where the brygge was next to the Inner warde', and in 'takyng up and losyng [losing] the same brigge'. The filled-in cavity has since formed part of the continuous path between the two wards.

The working of the middle gate drawbridge must have been controlled from inside the projecting porch. Originally a roofed structure, the gate covered the doorway to the corridor through which we now pass into the inner ward.

A detail from the bird's-eye view of Conwy produced about 1600 showing the roofed well and the middle gate (By permission of the marquess of Salisbury, Hatfield House, CPM I/62).

Opposite: A wide cleft was cut from north to south in the castle rock to isolate the approach to the inner ward. The castle well was formed at the centre of the cleft, and beyond it lay a drawbridge and the small, projecting inner gate.

Right: A view of the royal apartments of the inner ward from the battlements of the Chapel Tower. The L-shaped arrangement of the rooms is clearly visible, with the Great Chamber in the foreground.

The Inner Ward

The inner ward was the heart of the castle containing, as it did, the L-shaped suite of apartments which Master James of St George contracted to build for King Edward and Queen Eleanor in 1283 for £320, and the woodwork of which Master Richard of Chester and Master Henry of Oxford undertook to fashion for a further £100. The wording of the record makes it probable that these contracts also embraced the building of the great hall range in the outer ward. The king and queen's apartments occupied the south and east sides

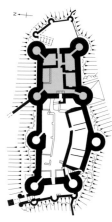

A reconstruction of the inner ward as it may have appeared at the end of the thirteenth century. The wooden staircases led up to the principal rooms on the first floor. The 'Presence Chamber' and 'Privy Chamber' (as they were identified in a survey of 1627) lay in the block on the right. To the left (east) was the 'Great Chamber' originally intended as the king's living room (Illustration by Terry Ball, 1990; with modifications 1998).

of the inner ward, facing inwards on to a small open quadrangle of which the outer sides are formed by the curtain walls. At one time the open area was even smaller, as there was a timber-framed building along most of the north side as well. Its foundation remains, as do the filled-in bearer-holes of its roof; it may be that this was the building called '*le gerner*' (the granary) and described in a survey of 1343 as being ruinous for want of its roof. It had apparently ceased to exist by the time of the 1627 survey. Further space must have been taken up by outside staircases, probably of wood and probably covered, to the doorways at first-floor level in the south-east and south-west corners. The east stair would have led up to a landing, called in Latin an *oriolum*, in front of what was the entrance to the king's Great Chamber; it may be that this is where we should look for the explanation for the payment of 20s. made in 1286 to Master Henry of Oxford 'for taking down the steps to the king's chamber and constructing an "oriel" in the middle of the castle' (*pro fractur' graduum camere regis in castro predicto et pro oriol' in medio castri ad tascham predicto H. traditam per dominum J. de Bonovillario et magistrum Jacobum*).

Only on two occasions in their history were these rooms actually occupied and used by the kings for whose accommodation they were built: by Edward I himself while grappling with the crisis of Madog's war over Christmas 1294 and the first few months of 1295; and by Richard II (1377–99) as the coming confrontation with Henry Bolingbroke, duke of Lancaster (d. 1413) moved towards its climax at Flint in the summer of 1399. On walking through Conwy's bare ruins, we may pause to reflect that it would have been in one of these very rooms that in February 1295 Archbishop-elect, Robert Winchelsey (1294–1313), took the oath of fealty to King Edward, at the end of his long, slow journey across the Alps to Italy and back to receive the *pallium* and secure the pope's confirmation of his election to the see of Canterbury. It was here, too, that Richard of Bordeaux received the 'tidings of calamity' (Shakespeare, *King Richard the Second*, Act III Scene II) that presaged the events at Flint and his captive progress to Chester and the Tower of London.

Above: In this late thirteenth-century manuscript illustration, Edward I faces a group of clergy led by an archbishop. Archbishop-elect, Robert Winchelsey, took the oath of fealty to Edward at Conwy in February 1295, probably in a chamber in the inner ward (By permission of the British Library, Cotton Vitellius Ms. A XIII, f. 6v).

Left: The tomb effigies of King Richard II (1377–99) and his queen, Anne (d. 1394), completed in 1398–99. Richard stayed at Conwy during the summer of 1399 and there received news of Henry Bolingbroke's efforts to seize the throne (Copyright: Dean and Chapter of Westminster).

The Royal Apartments

All of the residential rooms were on the upper floor and in the adjoining eastern towers. As we emerge from the passageway from the outer ward, we see facing us the remains of the beautiful traceried window of the principal room identified in the 1627 survey as '*a very faire one which is called the great chamber*' [1]. The Great Chamber was the king's living room, reached by way of the outside staircase to the doorway [2] in the corner of the inner ward, and also directly from the east barbican side by one of the narrow flights of steps in the thickness of the east curtain. This approach in turn allowed direct access between the Great Chamber and the water gate (p. 36) without any need to enter the castle proper at all; these steps also lead up to the private chapel in the Chapel Tower. On the river side, the chamber was lit by a group of three windows looking out over the garden in the east barbican. A grand

fireplace can be seen next to the window backing towards the courtyard.

From the Great Chamber a communicating door led southwards into the '*2 faire rooms*' identified by the 1627 survey as the 'Presence Chamber' [3] to the east, and the 'Privy Chamber' [4] to the west; the former has a single traceried window [5], the latter two matching windows [6], the three together forming the group facing northward on to the inner ward courtyard. There are further windows facing towards the Gyffin valley and Benarth Hill, and each chamber was fitted with a large fireplace in its northern wall. According to the survey, '*2 hansome withdrawinge roomes*' adjoined the west end of the Privy Chamber, but it is not easy to locate them unless they were upstairs in the Bakehouse Tower.

Floorless and roofless, these noble apartments now convey little impression of their original splendour. There is, however, one matter of structural interest that calls for comment. The walls of the inner ward display even more clearly than do

A general view of the inner ward — the heart of the castle — which contains the apartments built specifically for King Edward I and Queen Eleanor. The numbers on this view highlight the rooms and features described in the text on pages 28–31.

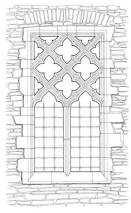
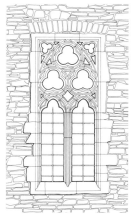

Far left: The courtyard-facing window of the Great Chamber as it appears today and a reconstruction of its tracery (Illustration by Chris Jones-Jenkins, after Toy 1936).

Left: The westernmost of the two courtyard-facing windows in the Privy Chamber and a reconstruction of its tracery (Illustration by Chris Jones-Jenkins, after Toy 1936).

those of the great hall (*magna aula*) tangible evidence of the entire replacement in the fourteenth century of the original open timber roofs of the 1280s. Not long after the creation of Edward of Woodstock, the Black Prince, as prince of Wales in 1343, orders were given (November 1346) to make the castle ready for four days' residence by the prince's auditors, and to provide bread, ale, flesh, fish, firewood, coal, hay, oats, litter and other things necessary to receive them. Within a few months, in 1347, further orders were given for 'repairing the arches of the hall of the castle', the stone to be quarried at Chester and shipped to Conwy by water. The record is not explicit and the accounts do not survive, but there can be little doubt that the works embraced the renewal of the roofs of the inner as well as the outer ward. Here, only one of the seven new arches remains intact, and is to be seen in the Privy Chamber [**7**].

Evidence of what happened can still be traced at several points. One of the clearest examples is in the Presence Chamber where, on the wall overlooking the Gyffin valley, to each side of the round-headed window embrasure, there are distinct marks of the thirteenth-century timber wall-posts left imprinted in the original plaster rendering. Below these marks, the replacement stone arches of 1347 are represented by the projecting springers that carried the masonry. Similarly, in the Great Chamber, to the left of the window looking out over the courtyard, one can still see — in its original position — a gritstone corbel that at first carried the wall-post supporting the open timber roof of about 1284. It was retained to carry the springer, no longer extant, of the new stone arch of the 1340s, of which the ragged seating hacked into the wall is all that now remains. Above this, in a

In the Presence Chamber, above either side of the round-headed window embrasure, there are distinct marks of the thirteenth-century timber wall-posts left imprinted in the original plaster rendering. The replacement stone arches of the 1340s are represented by the projecting springers set below.

A detail of one of the springers that supported the arches of the later roof over the Great Chamber.

vertical line with the original corbel, there is again the mark left in the rendering by the original wall-post. This and other similar surviving corbels are noteworthy as being exactly dated examples, and also as being explicitly connected by documentation with the name of James of St George (*Magistro Jacobo de Sancto Georgio … pro corbellis aule et camere regis*).

As to the basement rooms of the inner ward, it is only thanks to the 1627 survey that we are able to attribute any names, even if these are not particularly informative. Under the Great Chamber there was '*a litle roome used as a buttery*', and at the north end of it '*a large arched roome used for a Cellar*' [**8**]. The space below the Presence Chamber was described as '*a like large roome used for a Kitchen*' [**9**]; and that under the Privy Chamber '*a faire lowe Parlor*' (perhaps a servants' hall) [**10**]. This is the source of the names adopted on the ground-floor plan of the castle (inside back cover).

When the survey was taken in 1627, it was reported that '*the leads over all the roomes in this Court are in good state, and but litle broken, but the Timber that beares it, and the floares of the upper roomes are soe much decayed that one cannot goe into them without a double dainger of fallinge through the floare, and havinge the beames that hange loose above to fall upon his head*'.

The Towers of the Inner Ward

The King's Tower

On either side of the doorway to the east barbican straight flights of stairs lead up through the thickness of the east curtain wall. In the original plan they were the means by which the king and members of his suite, arriving at the castle by water, would ascend directly to the royal apartments on the main floor of the inner ward and in the two eastern towers. The south staircase (to the right as you leave the courtyard) connects with the bottom of the circular staircase of the tower traditionally known as the King's Tower. The circular staircase was reinstated in 1955 as far as wall-walk level, and from its landings we are able to see into the sites of the former rooms. The original floors and roofs, as in all towers,

have long since perished. The turret stairs have also been made good.

The King's Tower was of four storeys. The lowest was a basement entered only through a trap-door in the floor above; it is more likely to have been intended as a safe store for treasure than a prison. The first- and second-floor rooms were probably royal bed chambers. Each has a fine and well-preserved stone-hooded fireplace, and each drew its principal light from a two-light window, the distinctive round-headed embrasures of which are closely paralleled by examples at Harlech. The topmost room has a similar window but no fireplace and was, perhaps, assigned to servants.

The Chapel Tower

The northern (or left-hand) steps lead up similarly to the Chapel Tower. There is no historical authority for the tradition particularly associating this tower with Queen Eleanor. It is true that the accounts speak of James of St George executing the stonework for the hall and chambers of the king and queen, and also that the queen was at Conwy with Edward I for four months in 1283, and again for shorter spells in 1284, but in the first of these periods the building of the castle was only just beginning and in the second it

Opposite: The three large windows in the east-facing wall of the Great Chamber looked out over the river and the east barbican. To either side were the King's Tower and Chapel Tower, containing further royal apartments. A stepped ramp once led from the gap at the foot of the Chapel Tower down to the water gate. The line of the ramp is still detectable in the traces of the surface whitening on the turret in the foreground.

During the events that led to his abdication in 1399, King Richard II spent some time at Conwy. On the altar in the chapel royal, Henry Percy (d. 1408), earl of Northumberland, swore an oath of no treachery to the king. In this early fifteenth-century depiction of the scene, the king wears a black hood (By permission of the British Library, Harley Ms. 1319, f. 41v).

was still incomplete. When, ten years later, the king next came again to Conwy, to keep Christmas in the castle in 1294 and to reside there through the first six months of 1295, he came as a widower, Queen Eleanor having died in November 1290. In the accounts of the 1520s and 1530s, which are the earliest sources for any of the tower names, this tower is always called the Chapel Tower.

The name is derived from the little chapel royal which occupied the first floor, and the chancel of which, weathered and mutilated as it is, remains the most beautiful single feature in the castle. The main circle of the room formed the body of the chapel, the chancel being contrived in an apse-ended recess in the thickness of the eastern wall.

The sides of the recess are arcaded in seven bays, each of the three eastern of which is pierced by a lancet window in its upper tier. The lower part of each bay formed a trefoil-headed niche, the sides of which terminate in moulded wall-ribs carried up to the springing of the vaulted roof. At the lower level the arcading appears originally to have extended further to the west on either side; possibly this was so that the projecting ends might support a rood

beam: there is, indeed, a record of payment being made in 1286 for an image or figure bought in Chester 'for the chapel in the castle of Conway', but this may equally well have been for the main chapel in the outer ward (p. 20).

Entries concerning the chapel in 1533, when 4s. 7d. was paid 'to the bushop doffe for halowyng the aulter in the Castell', and 1535 when two locks were purchased 'for the closed dore in the chapell whear the vestmentes & other necessares belongyng to the same chapell do lye', probably also refer to the main chapel. The surveyors of 1627 speak of the generally decayed state of the floors and roofs of the other towers, but report that 'That in the Northeast corner is in the best repare, where there is a Chappell in the first storie into which one may goe safely, the floare of the chappell beinge reasounable good, and the Leades stanch above'.

It is no doubt because this tower was relatively well maintained well into the seventeenth century that the chapel and the chamber above it retain to this day so much of their original wall plaster. As in the King's Tower, the stairs in the Chapel Tower were renewed up to wall-walk level in 1955; in 1966 they were extended to the top of the surmounting turret. Since that date the tower has also been reroofed and refloored. An exhibition — Chapels in Castles — now occupies the basement and a model of Conwy as it may have looked at the beginning of the fourteenth century is located in the chamber above the chapel.

The Stockhouse Tower

The Henry VIII accounts contain several references to a tower, apparently in the inner ward, which was known at that time as the Stockhouse Tower. Probably the tower so-called was the one entered from the north-west corner of the courtyard. In the original thirteenth-century arrangement it may have contained guest rooms. The explanation of the sixteenth-century name, now adopted for it, appears from a record of 1519 for the payment of 6d. to sawyers at Cayrune (Caerhun) 'for Sawyng of xla fote of tymber for the makyng of two pares of Stocks for prisoners in the said Castell of Conway', and of 20d. to one Bartholomew Stodart 'for making the ironwork for the said stocks'. About the same time Stodart was paid 6d. 'for an Instrument called Manacles to sette appon the handes of felonnes in the said Castell'.

The tower contains a basement and two upper rooms. Its newel staircase remains unrestored, and

The Stockhouse Tower sits at the north-west corner of the inner ward, and comprises a basement and two upper rooms.

Conwy Castle (below right) in about 1811, painted in oil by William Daniell (1769–1837). Daniell's view shows the gaping hole in the Bakehouse Tower before it was repaired (© National Museums & Galleries of Wales). The dark patch of masonry in the lower part of the Bakehouse Tower (below) represents the repair effected in 1887.

visitors have therefore to view its interior either from the ground or from the level of the wall-walk. The basement, approached down six steps from the courtyard, will have been the room used in Tudor times as the 'stockhouse'. Each of the upper rooms contains the usual fireplace and an embrasure for a two-light window with window-seats. In 1534 each is recorded as being assigned to a Welsh prisoner, and bedsteads were provided for them: '*21d. payd for a bedcase for the chamber next over the stockhouse where Robert ap Willm lyeth; 20d. for a bedcase for the chamber next over the same chamber where Humffre ap Hol ap Jenkyn lyeth*'.

The Bakehouse Tower

The tower entered from the south-west corner of the inner ward appears to be that named in the sixteenth-century accounts as the Bakehouse Tower. It is of three storeys, the lowest of which contains a baking oven in the thickness of the wall. Alone of all the eight towers of the castle it is the one which has suffered major structural damage.

For this reason it was long known as the 'broken tower', and appears in the painting of Conwy by J. M. W. Turner (1775–1851), and in numerous nineteenth-century engravings, with a yawning hole extending nearly the full height of its outer side. The gap was repaired in 1887 by the London and North Western Railway Company, the new masonry then inserted being a conspicuous feature both inside and out.

The windows of the Great Chamber overlooked the lawned garden in the east barbican. The gateway to the inner ward was protected by a row of elaborate machicolations like that in the west barbican.

The East Barbican and Water Gate

Both in its purpose and in the essentials of its design the east barbican is a repetition of its western counterpart (pp. 17–18). It comprises a level forecourt in front of the passage which connects it to the inner ward, the opening being similarly protected from above by a row of elaborate machicolations, while on the opposite side the enclosure is similarly bounded by a low wall with three open-topped turrets which externally rise, or rather rose, sheer from the rocky edge of the river, their true footings being today concealed by the abutment of Telford's suspension bridge (1826).

The steep approach from the former postern or water gate comes up through a narrow gap between the northern turret and the Chapel Tower in the same way as the approach from within the town rises between the west barbican's northern turret and the north-west tower, a broad flight of steps leading almost directly up to the door in the east curtain (see plan inside back cover).

The east barbican is larger than the west and appears always to have served as a lawn or garden. It is so named (*herbarium*) in an account of 1316. In 1531 it is called '*the litell garden*', to distinguish it from '*the gret garden without the Castell*' which the late sixteenth-century drawing shows laid out with trees and formal beds on the ground now occupied by the car park between the castle and Mill Gate.

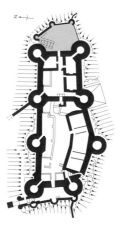

THE NORTH EAST VIEW OF CONWAY CASTLE, IN THE COUNTY OF CAERNARVON.

THIS Castle of Aber Conway pleads greater Antiquity than the Town; for it was fortified by Hugh Earl of Chester, in the Reign of William the Conqueror; but afterwards being damaged in the Wars, and falling to decay, was rebuilt by King Edwd. I. In ye beginning of the late Civil Wars Dr. John Williams Arch Bishop of York, a native of this Place, having made his Escape from Yorkshire hither, did at his own Expence fortify this Castle for the King, and held it till May 1645. when it was seized by Sr. John Owen, by virtue of a Commission from Prince Rupert; and on 19th January 1646. It was delivered up to the Parliament

Saml. & Nathl. Buck del. et sculp. Publish'd according to Act of Parliament April 5. 1742.

Above: The 1742 engraving of Conwy by Samuel and Nathaniel Buck provides some of the best evidence for the form of the water gate at the east end of the castle.

Right: The east barbican, containing 'the litell garden' with trees and formal beds, and the water gate as depicted in the anonymous bird's-eye view of Conwy of about 1600 (By permission of the marquess of Salisbury, Hatfield House, CPM I/62).

The water gate, or postern, no longer exists. Originally it was the most important feature of this end of the castle, and no description would be complete without some account of it. This must necessarily be based in the main on evidence that can be deduced from the late sixteenth-century bird's-eye view of Conwy and the print of 1742 by Samuel and Nathaniel Buck. Neither representation approached photographic accuracy, but it is clear that from the gate in the gap beside the Chapel Tower a stepped ramp curved down and round, flanked by its own lesser turrets and hugging the barbican wall, to a

point on the rocks somewhere near the foot of the middle barbican turret — that is, beneath the end of Telford's suspension bridge. The earlier picture shows a low broken wall continuing still further southwards along the base of the rocks; possibly it went on to join an outlying round tower, known to have been begun and possibly never finished, which stood near the water's edge to the south-east of the castle. The sloping line of the ramp has left its mark on the outside of the turret next to the Chapel Tower, the wall face which it formerly covered being free of the surface whitening still noticeable higher up (p. 30).

Another outlying round tower is first mentioned in the year 1298, when William Thornton, mason, was paid 60s. for quarrying and dressing stone 'for a new tower which the king has ordained to be made between the castle and the water'. In 1343, surveyors reported that an unfinished tower, which from the description is almost certainly this one, could be completed for £60, when it was said it would stand the castle in very great stead. It seems possible that this is the tower shown standing in front of the water gate approach in the sixteenth-century view.

The Wall-Walks and Battlements

The tops of the curtain walls are accessible to visitors and may be reached by the stairs in all but the Kitchen and Stockhouse Towers. Many points of interest are visible from the upper level.

The purpose of the wall-walks was to provide a continuous sentry-path round the whole castle and to give ready access to the roofs of the buildings which almost everywhere stood against the curtains. In time of siege, all available defence could be concentrated on the wall-head above the threatened sector, and timber screens or hourds built out from the battlements so as actually to overhang an enemy who gained the wall-foot. The ends of the slots or grooves provided to carry the bearers of these hourds can be seen throughout the castle, one below each arrowloop on towers and curtains alike.

The tops of the walls, like those of the buildings against them, were covered with lead, and evidence of this remains in the creasing, to be seen at the base of the parapets and towers all round the wall-walks, from which the lead flashings have been torn away. The creasing has the appearance of having been cut at a later date than the first building of the walls, and may result from the general reroofing of the castle buildings effected in the time of the Black Prince — about 1346 (p. 7). The isolation of the inner ward could be maintained at wall-walk as well as at courtyard level; on the sides of the Stockhouse and Bakehouse Towers can be seen rebates for doors which could be used for shutting off the inner ward wall-walks from the rest.

The stairs in six of the towers have been restored above wall-walk level, enabling us to see at close quarters the great height of the merlons, the alternating levels of the arrowloops, the cresting, the pinnacles, and what is left of some of the stone chimney stacks and drainage outlets. Those in the three inner ward towers have been extended to the tops of the turrets.

The rebate on the side of the Stockhouse Tower represents a door used to shut off the inner ward wall-walks from the rest of the castle.

The wall-walks provided a continuous sentry-path round the whole castle. This section to the south of the great hall range shows the Prison Tower in the foreground, with the south-west tower beyond.

The Town Walls

The town walls of Conwy constitute the finest and most completely preserved example of their class of monument left in Britain. Nowhere else are there town walls of such extent built in a single operation and surviving so little altered and in such completeness. They have the added interest that we know exactly when they were built and even the names and background of some of the building masters whose employees worked on them.

The purpose of the walls was to enclose and protect the new chartered town founded in 1284, and at the same time to afford, on the landward side, a strong forward defence to the castle itself. So much, indeed, were castle and fortified town regarded as a single conception that during the period March–June 1283, when both were still in the stage of site preparation, the day-to-day accounts more than once refer to their whole area as the *castrum*, instead of distinguishing, as they generally do, between the *castrum* (castle) and the *villa* (town).

The walls were built simultaneously with the castle, and a contemporary record shows that their construction was well advanced by the autumn of 1286. Payment was made at this time for:

i   Battlementing and whitening the battlements of the five towers (Towers 17–21) and six lengths of wall on either side of the Mill Gate;

ii   Battlementing and other works on the towers of the Mill Gate and for making the twelve corbelled projections on the wall to the west of it (p. 56);

iii Works on a spur wall closing the quay and on the round tower which stood out in the river at the end of it;

iv   For the voussoirs and jambs of the postern gate in this spur wall;

v   Digging out the rock-cut ditch which fronted the walls along the north-west side of the town.

Probably there was little if any pause in the work, though there are structural indications that some of the towers with their adjacent stairs (such as Tower 5) were first built to wall-walk height in advance of the intervening stretches of wall; that in some places (for example, Towers 5, 6 and 7) there was at least a slight break in building before the towers were continued above that level; and, lastly, that the upper part of the spur wall was not built until later.

The building of the walls, as of the castle, was under the overall direction of James of St George as 'Master of the King's Works in Wales'. Among the building masters named in the 1286 accounts as responsible for particular tasks and contracts in connection with them are four men from abroad — John Francis, believed like Master James to have come from Savoy and later found working with him at Beaumaris; Jules of Chalons; William of Seyssel (from Seyssel on the Rhone); and Peter of Boulogne; and three with English names — Roger of Cockersand, from the Cistercian abbey of that name on the

Left: The little castle and town walls at Saillon were built in 1262 for Count Peter of Savoy (d. 1268). The design details at this Swiss site bear a marked resemblance to the style and workmanship typical of Conwy some twenty years later. This view shows a stretch of the Saillon walls punctuated by uniform towers, a feature which is also very striking at Conwy (Peter Humphries).

A cast of the earliest known Conwy borough seal, probably dating to about 1316 (Society of Antiquaries).

Opposite: The full extent of Conwy's town walls and the mastery of their design are best appreciated from Tower 13 which rises high above the Edwardian borough and castle.

There were up to 480 loopholes in the circuit of the town walls, designed for defence with crossbows. One of the best preserved is found on Tower 15 (above). In this fourteenth-century manuscript illustration (below) a man is shown loading a crossbow (By permission of the British Library, Additional Ms. 42130, f. 56).

Lancashire coast; John of Sherwood, from Nottinghamshire; and Robert of Frankby, from the Wirral. The ditchers include English names such as Barber, Roden, Macclesfield, Kingston and Gedling, besides Thomas Picard from across the Channel.

The walls were designed to meet possible attack in a particular way. This was to create a barrier of masonry so strong that it could not be breached and which, while presenting a continuous front to the enemy without, was so sectioned within as automatically to isolate any scaling party that might succeed in obtaining a foothold on its summit.

Each of the flanking towers, spaced at roughly 50 yard (46m) intervals along the whole length of the walls, was so designed as to act as it were as a circuit-breaker between one section and the next, continuity of the wall-walk across the towers' open gorges being maintained by simple plank bridges which could easily be destroyed or removed by the defenders in the event of a serious threat developing at any one point. With the bridges removed, each tower, together with the section of wall extending on one side of it, formed a self-contained unit of defence. Originally, therefore, there had to be a flight of steps from the street level to the wall-walk beside nearly every tower, with a steep little winding stair leading on from near the top of the steps to the battlements of the tower itself. There would have been no access, in the absence of the bridges, to the next adjoining section of the wall.

There is an exception in the case of the westernmost tower (13) which, being circular, was not open-gorged and therefore needed no bridge; this tower could, accordingly, be reached both from the stairs beside Tower 12 and from those beside the Upper Gate, while the steps to its battlements curve up against its inside face. There are still substantial remains of no fewer than eleven of the main flights of stairs as well as traces of some of the others.

The whole circuit of walls and towers was crowned with loopholed battlements, the loops being pierced, like those on the castle and at Harlech and Beaumaris, with perfect regularity and at alternating elevations. Except along the quayside, a great deal of this battlementing remains. A rough calculation shows that altogether it must have provided, with the loops in the towers, something like 480 loopholes; to man those of one average section with its associated tower would have

required eighteen to twenty men. Possibly a small reserve of crossbows, and of the quarrels and bolts used for their ammunition, would originally have been kept in the lower part of each tower.

When the bridges were in position, watchmen could patrol the battlements from one end of the walls to the other, and in times of peril we may be sure they did so. We read for example how at Caernarfon, where the walls, though of less extent, were a replica of their Conwy contemporaries, a wage of 4d. a night was paid throughout the summer months of 1384 and 1385 to Richard Ince 'for doing night by night his vigils on the walls of the town,

because of persistent rumours touching war, rapine, murder and arson and the Scottish enemies of the lord king and his lieges in North Wales'. The maintenance of the walls and their woodwork remained of importance until Tudor times. An account of 1523–24 records payment of 30s. *'to the Prior of Ruthlan for xiiij peces of tymber to make thereof plankes for the Briges appon the town Walles of Conwey'* and of 4s. to carpenters for *'wrykynge appon the settynge of the said planks brige wise appon the said Walles'*, one John Alderleigh being allowed to have *'thold tymbr of thold briges'* for 3s. 5d.

The bridges would not have been the only woodwork in the walls as originally completed. At wall-walk level each tower had a timber floor, carried on the offset which can still be seen, giving access to three embrasures whose loopholes commanded the approach to the walls from every angle. Whether or not the towers, other than Tower 16 (p. 54), were roofed remains uncertain. Provision was also made for equipping the walls with timber hourds, the beam holes for which can be seen throughout their length below the arrowloops and the timbers for which may have been stored in the lower part of the towers.

An impression of Conwy as it may have appeared in the early fourteenth century. As at Caernarfon, or at Denbigh, the town was part and parcel of King Edward's military settlement of north Wales. At Conwy, the walls rose with those of the castle itself, and by 1314 there were 124 'burgage plots' (tenements) situated within the town defences (Illustration by Ivan Lapper, 1990).

The Town Walls Itinerary

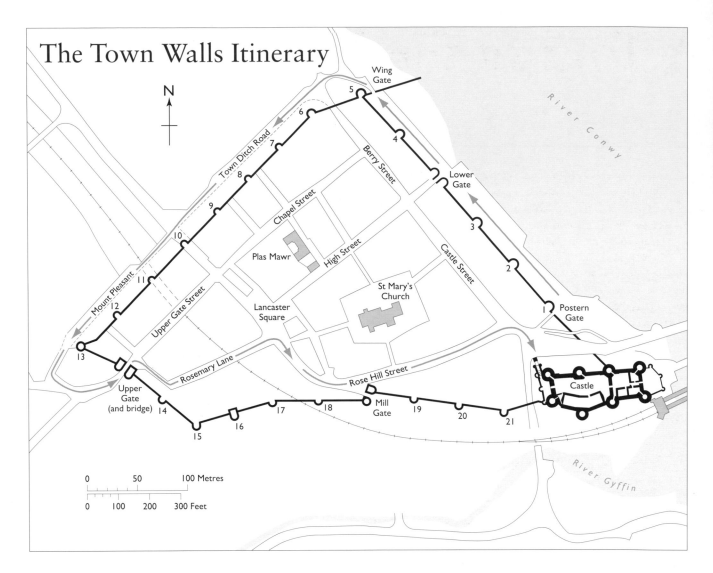

Those who wish to follow the itinerary of the town walls will find the following a convenient route.

Quayside Section
On leaving the castle, cross the road to the postern gate beside Tower 1 and pass under the arch to the quayside. Follow the quay road as far as the arch through the spur wall at the foot of Tower 5.

Town Ditch and Mount Pleasant Section
Pass through the arch, bear left up the hill and proceed along Town Ditch Road. Cross Bangor Road, which was driven through the base of Tower 10 in 1827, and follow Mount Pleasant as far as Tower 13. This marks the western extremity and highest point of the medieval town, and furnishes excellent views of the entire town and the castle.

Upper Gate and Gyffin Sections
Beyond Tower 13, turn left and follow the road down through the Upper Gate into the town. Turn right into Rosemary Lane, from which views can be obtained of the inside of the walls between the Upper Gate and Tower 17. At the end of Rosemary Lane turn right into Rose Hill Street and continue along it past the Mill Gate to the castle.

Panorama
For the best panorama of the town and castle, you should leave the walled town by way of the Mill Gate, follow the subway under the railway, and cross the car park to Benarth Road; turn left and cross to the kissing-gate on the right; take the footpath up the Benarth Hill towards the woods. As the path rises, the whole extent of the castle and walled town comes into view across the valley.

A Tour of the Town Walls

The town walls are approximately 1,400 yards (1.3km) in length, and are flanked by twenty-one towers and pierced by three double-towered gateways (see The Town Walls Itinerary opposite). In addition, there is a spur or wing wall projecting some 60 yards (55m) from the end of the quay and formerly terminating in a round tower which stood out in the water. The tower was still standing about 1600, as shown in the picture on page 8. For purposes of description the walls may be conveniently dealt with in four main sections:

1 Quayside Section
2 Town Ditch and Mount Pleasant Section
3 Upper Gate Section
4 Gyffin Section

Quayside: Castle to Tower 5

The town walls commence against the Stockhouse Tower on the north side of the castle. This arrangement was evidently deliberate, for the Stockhouse Tower marks the junction of the inner with the outer ward and the part of the castle containing the royal quarters was accordingly isolated from contact with the town. For a short distance, where the wall is on the castle rock and where it begins to cross the site of the castle ditch, it is a simple screen wall only 3 feet (91cm) in thickness and without parapet or wall-walk. Once across the ditch, it assumes the character and dimensions — the normal thickness is about 5 feet

Conwy Castle and the quayside section of the town walls from a drawing made about 1846 by W. H. Bartlett (1809–54), engraved by J. C. Armytage (1820–97). The drawing predates the construction of the tubular railway bridge in 1848 (By permission of the National Library of Wales).

The junction of the town walls with the defences of the castle at the base of the Stockhouse Tower. The stretch of wall that crossed the castle ditch was a simple screen wall only some 3 feet (91cm) thick and devoid of battlements.

The spur wall and the now-vanished round tower at its end in a detail from the late sixteenth-century view of Conwy (By permission of the marquess of Salisbury, Hatfield House, CPM I/62).

6 inches (1.68m) — which mark it throughout the remainder of its length. The nearest tower to the castle is not a medieval structure, but an imitation built by Thomas Telford in 1826 beside a gate made to give access to his new suspension bridge; this gate, and with it the point of junction between the two thicknesses of medieval wall, was demolished in 1958.

If you are following the suggested itinerary, you should cross the road opposite the castle and pass through the wall by the postern gate on to the quay. The postern is a simple opening, designed for an ordinary door without portcullis; flanked and protected by the adjacent Tower 1 and under observation from the castle itself, it did not need to be strongly defended. Its purpose was to provide access to the outer-ward end of the castle from the ferry across the river Conwy just as the castle's own water gate did at the inner-ward end.

The quayside towers (numbers 1 to 4) have suffered severely. All have lost their battlemented

parapets, and most have had their arrowloops gouged out to make windows for dwellings, which in times past have been intruded into their interiors. Indeed, much of the stretch of wall between Tower 2 and Tower 5, though surviving structurally intact, is hidden behind buildings. The twin-towered Lower Gate, through which many a cargo of water-borne supplies and goods for the town must have passed into Conwy at all periods from the thirteenth to the twentieth century, has suffered equally with the wall towers. In its original appearance it must have closely resembled the Upper and Mill Gates.

The quayside is bounded towards the north by a wall 10 feet 6 inches (3.1m) thick — double the normal thickness — which runs down across the foreshore; now generally known as the spur wall, it takes the form of a prolongation of the alignment of the Tower 5 to Tower 6 section of the main wall. Though broken off at the end, it retains most of its original length. The 1286 building account shows that the spur wall, then being erected, terminated in a round tower which stood out in the water towards Deganwy. Indeed, the account refers to it as the '*turris rotunda in mare de Conewey propinquiori le Gannou*'. Such a use of *mare* (sea) for 'river' recalls the name '*Entre Deux Mers*' given to the district between the rivers Garonne and Dordogne in Gascony.

It seems likely that this wall and tower were already in danger of succumbing to the force of the waters within twenty years or so of their erection, and no doubt it is this threat that is referred to in an early fourteenth-century petition in which the 'poor burgesses of Conwy' beseech the king to assign £20 a year towards the cost of works needed 'to save the wall and towers of the town, which are in great peril from the tides of the river' (*pur sauvacion du Mur et des tours de la dite vile qe sunt en grant peril pur les*

Elevation Drawing of the Castle and Town Walls (Castle to Tower 5)

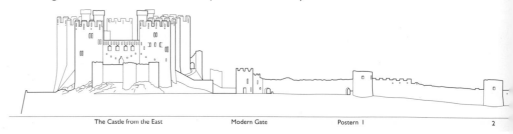

The Castle from the East   Modern Gate   Postern 1   2

vades de la Mier). If, as seems probable, the spur wall was conceived as much as a breakwater as a military defence, intended to form a haven and to protect the foundations of the main wall along the quayside from the under-scour of high tides and stormy seas, its maintenance would have been vitally important, and it was probably in this same connection that a seven-year murage grant had already been made to the burgesses in 1305, some few years before the date of the petition quoted.

We have already noted (p. 39) that there are structural indications that the upper part of the spur wall is later than the lower. Not merely is it straight-jointed against Tower 5, but in order to give access to its wall-walk one of the original arrowloop embrasures of the tower, after first being built in the usual form, has been enlarged on one side and blocked up on the other. Moreover the spur wall-walk and the main wall-walk are at markedly different levels. Probably, therefore, the lower 12 feet (3.7m) or thereabouts are original work of the 1280s, and

the remainder a building-up effected in the second decade of the fourteenth century. The stone of the later work is, very largely, the brownish rhyolite seen also in the upper parts of adjacent sections of the main wall; this is the rock of which the nearby Bodlondeb Hill is composed, and probably it was there that the stone was quarried.

The wide wall-walk has a looped parapet on either side, that towards the town having loops in alternate merlons only. To allow communication between the quayside and the ground outside the walls to the north and west there was a gate in the spur wall close beside Tower 5; this has been widened in modern times, but its portcullis groove remains on one side, while over the gate arch there is a large rectangular shaft for the counterweight. The spur wall was an integral part of the medieval plan for the defence of the town and maintenance of its harbour; but it is in a vulnerable position, and for so much of it to have survived the vicissitudes of storm and plunder is remarkable.

The spur wall at the north end of the quayside was probably designed as much as a breakwater as a military defence.

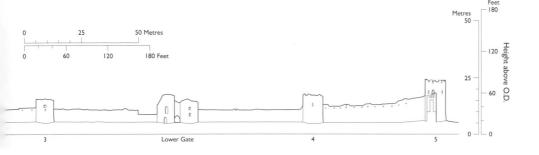

A watercolour of the town walls and castle by Moses Griffith (1747–1819), Griffith's view shows Tower 13 in the foreground, with the Town Ditch and Mount Pleasant section of the walls to the left, and the Upper Gate section to the right (Private collection).

Town Ditch and Mount Pleasant: Tower 5 to Tower 13

From the northernmost corner of the town at Tower 5 the wall leaves the riverside and runs steeply uphill on an alignment which is followed only as far as Tower 6, a distance of a little under 60 yards (55m). At Tower 6 the main north-west alignment begins, and from here to Tower 13 a straight course is maintained for very nearly ¼ mile (400m). The outward aspect of this unbroken stretch of wall, with its battlements and nine symmetrically spaced flanking towers, provides one of the most imposing and impressive pieces of medieval town fortification in Britain.

Visitors who follow the suggested itinerary of the walls (p. 42) will find their general layout and character particularly easy to comprehend along this section, and comment may be made on a number of points likely to attract notice. Originally, the section contained no gates or posterns. Today, a little way beyond Tower 5, there are modern openings through the wall at the end of Berry Street, the first of five such breaches on this side of the town. Happily they have been restricted to arches through the lower part of the wall, the continuity of which, after some 700 years, still remains unbroken throughout the upper levels. On either side of the Berry Street openings it has been possible to reconstitute sections

Elevation Drawing of the Town Walls (Tower 5 to Tower 13)

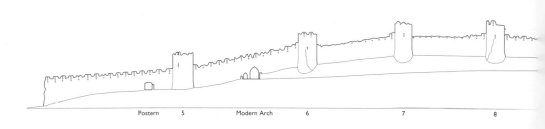

Postern   5   Modern Arch   6   7   8

of the bank upon which the walls originally stood and
to excavate and expose part of the accompanying
defensive ditch.

The wall continues to climb, though not quite so
steeply, as far as Tower 7. Up to this point it will be
noticed that much use is made of the yellowish-
brown rhyolite stone employed for the spur wall and,
to a lesser extent, in the upper parts of the wall and
towers facing the quay. It is evident that Tower 5 and
its associated stair were built up to wall-walk level
in the predominant grit stone, before the walls to
the north-east and south-west of it and its own
uppermost stage were added in the contrasting
material. Tower 6 shows a similar change of building
stone from a point a little above the wall-walk, while
between it and Tower 7 one or two courses of
rhyolite appear at wall-walk level immediately below
the parapet. Tower 7 also exhibits a change of build,
though not in this case of material, from wall-walk
level upwards, the top storey being faced with larger
and more regularly coursed blocks of Silurian grit
than those characteristically found in the lower levels.
Beyond Tower 7 practically no rhyolite is seen.

The inference to be drawn from all this appears to
be that, in this quarter at any rate, there was an initial
stage of building which comprised only the lower part
of a tower, together with its stair and the adjoining
section of wall against which the stair ascended; a
second stage saw the erection of the rest of the wall
linking tower to tower and of the upper part of the
towers themselves; finally, the battlemented parapets
were added and, as we know from the accounts,
finished with protective 'daub' or rendering. The
stages of construction are less easy to see where
they are not emphasized by a difference of building
material, and it is not certain that they were
consistently followed through the circuit of the walls.

*The upper part of Tower 6, with
its well-preserved battlements
and very distinctive change in
the use of building stone just
above wall-walk level.*

Right: The projecting stone near the top of Tower 8 may have been used to suspend a plumb-bob to align the adjacent length of town wall during construction.

Opposite: Seen from the highest point at Tower 13, the Town Ditch Road and Mount Pleasant section of the town walls presents one of the most imposing and impressive pieces of medieval town fortifications in the whole of the British Isles.

The building of the Chester and Holyhead Railway in 1846 caused Tower 11 to subside, resulting in a large vertical fracture.

There are, however, a number of other places where it can be plainly seen that the building of the towers preceded, if only by a little, that of the walls between them (for example, against Towers 8, 14 and 15), and that the wall parapet was constructed separately from the main fabric below (for example, between the same two towers).

Towers 7, 8, 9, 10, 11 and 12, all have, or had, a single projecting stone high up on their south-west side, the purpose of which may have been to suspend a plumb-bob on the line to which the adjacent length of wall would need to conform when the builders came to add it against the tower.

Tower 6 is finely preserved. Besides the normal three cross-loops at wall-walk height, four similar loops, set at alternating levels, survive in the battlements. Not until we reach Tower 13 do we find another tower that has retained its battlements more or less intact. The opening of the coast road to Bangor in 1827 created a new axis across the line of the wall which has ever since tended to split the observer's appreciation of the inherent unity of this long north-west section. Until that year Tower 10 stood not as a gateway but as an ordinary wall tower, no different from those on either side of it. Telford brought his road straight up to the tower, across the then still open ditch, pierced it with a lofty arch and added the

castellated forework with its pseudo-machicolation. The subsequent carrying of the wall-walk on a bridge round the outer face of the tower on top of Telford's ornamental piers was the reverse of the medieval arrangement. We may be grateful, however, that Telford's instinct was to adapt the tower, not to demolish it, so preserving for posterity the full continuity of the medieval towered enceinte. A bridge has been constructed across the inner face at wall-walk level.

Tower 11 has likewise suffered as a result of nineteenth-century traffic development. The tunnel cut for the Chester and Holyhead Railway in 1846 passes almost directly beneath it and has caused a partial subsidence; this has led to considerable vertical fracturing of the masonry, but there is no evidence of recent movement, and in 1962–63 the tower was underpinned and carefully consolidated.

From here to the top of the town the ditch which fronted the wall in medieval times is filled up and is now used as a car park, and therefore not seen to its best advantage. The section between Towers 12 and 13 affords a good illustration of the method employed, already noted at the castle, of constructing the walls with the aid of inclined scaffold lifts up which heavy loads of stone could be hauled as the work progressed; no fewer than four sloping lines of putlog holes are here visible.

Tower 13 exhibits to perfection the same technique in its helicoidal form, the putlog holes spiralling round the face in the most striking fashion. No less noteworthy is the siting of the tower. Perched on a crag of rock, its position was chosen to enable it to dominate the town spread out below, and before the days of high buildings there can scarcely have been any point along the wall tops, from castle back to castle, that could not have been seen by a watchman posted on Tower 13. Further, by a masterly stroke of planning, the main wall lines to north-east and south-east are set a little back from the course required had they merely been aligned to meet a common-form corner tower at right-angles in the orthodox manner. Tower 13 is thereby endowed with an unbroken view straight down the ditch as far as Tower 6 in one direction and Tower 15 in the other; in particular it is given a dominating position in relation to the approaches to the Upper Gate, through which ran the only landward entry to medieval Conwy. Tower 13 is indeed the culminating point of the whole wall system.

Upper Gate:
Tower 13 to Tower 15

From Tower 5 to Tower 13, a distance of ¹/₄ mile (400m), the walls have made their long, gradual ascent from the river; now, from Tower 13 to Tower 15, a distance of 170 yards (155m), they descend rapidly again by an even gradient to the valley of the Gyffin. The section comprises three wall lengths, with the Upper Gate and Tower 14 dividing them. Of the four sectors into which the walls are

grouped for the purposes of this description, this one is architecturally the most impressive and structurally the best preserved.

The twin-towered Upper Gate is the section's principal feature. Referred to in the Middle Ages as '*the High Yate of Conwey*', it formed the main entrance to the town and was accordingly elaborately defended. The approach to it lay over a drawbridge across the rock-cut ditch, which continued along this part of the walls. The outward abutment of the bridge was protected by a barbican, part of the south wall of which, with four small loops, remains standing on the right-hand side of the road.

Elevation Drawing of the Town Walls (Tower 13 to Tower 15)

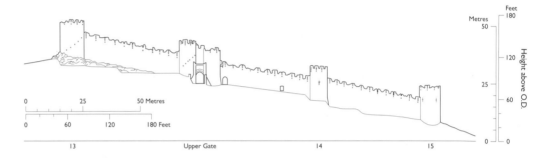

Below: From Tower 13, in the Upper Gate section, the town walls descend rapidly to the valley of the Gyffin, making a sharp turn at Tower 15 in the foreground of this view.

Evidence of the bridge itself may be seen in the rectangular housing into which it was drawn up flush against the outer archway of the gate, while the rounded stone seating in which its great wooden axle pivoted is visible some few feet above the modern roadway. As can easily be seen, the passageway through the gate was originally a level one which has been subsequently sloped and lowered — at the inner end by as much as 7 feet (2.1m) — for the greater convenience of modern wheeled traffic.

The medieval accounts contain several references to the repair of the bridge. In 1396 carpenters were paid for sawing great timbers 'for the high bridge on the south side of the town of Conway'. In 1520 a great piece of timber 'for the makyng of the axill of the said brige', and two 30 feet (9m) pieces 'for the shafts

Above: The heavily-defended Upper Gate, with the surviving wall of its barbican to the right. The gate formed the main entrance to the town and was accordingly elaborately defended.

Left: The medieval building accounts for Conwy contain several references to the repair of the Upper Gate drawbridge. Carpenters were at work on great timbers for the bridge in 1396, and the woodwork required more attention in 1520. In this detail from an early fourteenth-century manuscript, carpenters are shown at work sawing great timbers (By permission of the British Library Royal Ms. 10 E IV, f. 99v).

A section of the multiple corbelling between the Upper Gate and Tower 14.

unraised portcullis in front. From this platform the drawbridge itself was worked; a pair of recesses cut into the bottom course of its now destroyed parapet shows where the chains or ropes of the bridge were taken through to the winding gear.

The porter who controlled all these arrangements was accommodated in an L-shaped apartment which filled the whole of the back of the gatehouse and its southern tower at first-floor level. Its rearward wall, as with the other two Conwy gatehouses, was of timber, and rested on the flat arch which still spans the inner end of the gate-passage. The timbering was the work of Master Laurence of Canterbury, who in 1286 was paid £15 0s. 0d. 'for making the great gate and the chamber over the gate towards Caernarfon'.

The chamber was reached by way of the outside staircase (now partially rebuilt) which rises against the back and side of the southern tower and also gave access to the section of wall-walk between the gate and Tower 14. In the angle between the wall and the gate-tower are the remains of the porter's latrine. A separate room in the upper part of the northern tower appears to have been accessible only from the wall-walk and adjacent wall-stair on that side of the gate; from it stone steps lead up across the portcullis control box to give access to the battlements. The ground floor of both towers was occupied by guard chambers entered through barred doors in their back walls. The whole gatehouse is ingeniously planned and repays study.

From the Upper Gate the wall continues its descent to the valley of the Gyffin, the section terminating for practical purposes at Tower 15, where there is a sharp change of alignment.

The battlements of Towers 14 and 15 and of the intervening wall lengths are well preserved, wanting only their copings and finials. Indeed the outward view of this whole Upper Gate section, riding the slope and visible as a unified architectural conception, is one of the most exciting of the prospects of Conwy.

We now pass through the Upper Gate to see the inner side of the wall and towers from Rosemary Lane. Here a characteristic feature of the construction, not previously mentioned, will be noticed. This is the multiple corbelling which both enables the width of the wall-walk to exceed that of the wall below it and also serves to prevent surface water from dripping directly down the wall face.

of the said bridge', were brought 10 miles (16km) by water to Conwy — one David ap Res being paid 1s. 0d. 'for drawyng of the said axil tree and the said trees of xxxti fote longe from the water side at Conwey unto the said brige by his oxen'.

After passing the barbican and the bridge, incomers to the town were confronted with further obstacles. Ahead was an iron-plated portcullis, the medieval equivalent of the sliding door, the grooves for which remain on either side of the roadway; immediately beyond this again were the heavy two-leaved wooden doors, whose hinge and drawbar holes can also still be seen. The space between drawbridge and portcullis could be observed from either side through peep-holes in the flanking towers. No doubt the timber platform over it, beddings for the joists of which are visible in the cross-wall above, and to which there was access from a door in the side of the southern tower, contained murder holes or *meurtrières* which would constitute an added hazard to the stranger without the gate, caught as he might well be between the Scylla of a reraised drawbridge behind him and the Charybdis of an

Gyffin: Tower 15 to the Castle

The fourth and last section of the wall fronting towards the Conwy's tributary, the Gyffin, runs in a general west to east direction to rejoin the south-west corner of the castle. Its central feature is the Mill Gate, on either side of which are three wall towers (16 to 18, 19 to 21). Its length, from Tower 15 to the castle, is 385 yards (352m). It may properly be said to begin some 27 feet (8m) to the east of Tower 15, where a break in the masonry — the only break of its kind in the whole circuit of the wall — is visible on both the inner and the outer faces. This marks the eastern termination of the first work (1283–84), which comprised the whole length of the northern and western walls with the lower part of the spur wall and its now vanished water-tower. The southern wall, from here to the castle, was erected in 1286, the eastern wall facing the waterfront probably in 1287.

The break also coincides with the western end of a building, now destroyed but evidently originally of some importance, of which the wall itself, for a length of 85 feet (26m), formed the south side. Because of the former presence of this building, the wall is here pierced by three single-light windows with window-seated embrasures. These can be identified with three windows 'in the stretch of wall by the tower facing the Gyffin' for the making of which Philip de Derle, mason, is recorded as having been paid 30s. in 1286; for not only is the number correct, but no other stretch of the wall contains or has contained windows at all.

The building they lighted is likely to be that which the same record refers to as the 'new high chamber' (*nova camera elevata*), for its site is an elevated one in relation both to the land outside the wall and also to the ground in front of Tower 16. It belonged to an important group of buildings known collectively, at least as early as 1302, as Llywelyn's Hall, and therefore presumably dating from before the English

In the section of wall between Tower 15 (left) and Tower 16 (right), the three windows represent the position of Llywelyn's Hall. Tower 16 was much altered in 1305, when it was raised in height, and an enclosing back wall built.

conquest. A reference in the accounts of 1286 to 'three chambers in the hall which is called the Prince's Hall' no doubt relates to the same group. This hall may well have been the scene of the meetings at which, in November 1277, the king's and the prince's councillors drew up the armistice terms which concluded the first phase of King Edward's contest with Llywelyn.

Much work was done both on the buildings of Llywelyn's Hall, which have disappeared, and on the adjacent tower (16), which survives, in the years 1302–06. The roof of the hall was repaired and new locks provided for its doors; a new chapel was built, the freestone dressings for which were brought by water from Anglesey and Caernarfon.

The buildings that lay just inside the walls between Towers 15 and 16 were known collectively as Llywelyn's Hall. This reconstruction of the hall is based on an archaeological excavation of the site (Illustration by Terry Ball, 1998).

At the same time the tower itself was much altered, and the evidence of the alterations remains. As originally built in 1286 it was, like the other wall towers, open-gorged, and comprised the usual two stages with battlemented wall-top approached from the main wall-walk by steps on its western side; its position at a break in the wall's alignment meant, however, that the eastern side of its D-plan was more than usually prolonged. In 1305 the tower was raised in height, and close examination of its exterior shows that much of its upper part is in fact an early rebuilding. The back wall built to close its northern face is also of this date. Within, it was converted for residential use by the insertion of two floors, the principal accommodation being on the first floor. At this level the rounded end, which remains above and below, was cut away to give a room of more ample proportions and convenient shape, a room also provided with a good hooded fireplace and two well-built windows. The room above it is presumably the 'topmost solar' (*supremum solarium*) for which six tie-beams were provided. For the roof 4,000 shingles were made.

Though the documents leave no doubt that 'Llywelyn's Hall' lay in its vicinity, the tower itself is an Edwardian structure contemporary in date with the rest of the town wall, and the name 'Llywelyn's Tower' sometimes given to it is therefore strictly speaking a misnomer. In 1315 the hall proper, which was of timber, was dismantled, and removed by water to Caernarfon, where it was re-erected inside the castle.

The building of the Chester and Holyhead Railway in 1847 inevitably affected the appearance of the whole stretch of the walls between Tower 17 and the castle, the construction of the embankment destroying the impressiveness of defences designed

Elevation Drawing of the Castle and Town Walls (Tower 15 to the Castle)

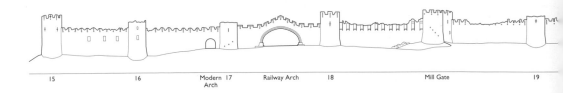

| 15 | 16 | Modern 17
Arch | Railway Arch | 18 | Mill Gate | 19 |

The Mill Gate differs from all of the other twin-towered gateways to be seen at Edward I's castles and walled towns in north Wales in that its towers do not form a pair.

to rise sheer from the margin of the stream. Between Towers 17 and 18 a great flattened four-centred arch was pierced and an imitation wall-walk and battlements built over it, a little above the correct level, in order to preserve the enceinte. But, when there might so easily have been indiscriminate destruction, posterity can be grateful to the railway builders for their skilful and considerate handling of the problem which the presence of the castle and walls at this particular spot posed for them.

Mill Gate spans the way into the former railway goods yard from Rose Hill Street. Before the building

of the railway the road through it led down to the Gyffin stream. Here from the earliest days of the borough's history was the king's water mill, from which the gate took its name. The placing of the gate at this point, and likewise its setting astride the wall instead of in alignment with it, must have been dictated by pre-existing conditions, such perhaps as an opening in a former precinct wall of the abbey to give access to the mill in the days when it had belonged to the monks.

The Mill Gate, with the stretch of wall adjoining it on the west, presents features of exceptional interest.

The railway arch between Towers 17 and 18, constructed in 1847.

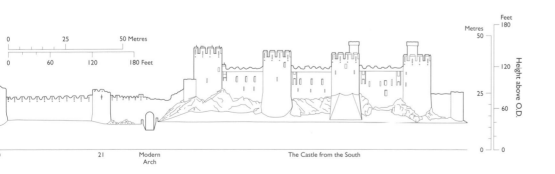

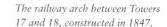

The pair of polygonal towers that flank the King's Gate at Caernarfon Castle.

Below: Between the Mill Gate and Tower 18, no fewer than twelve privies were corbelled out from the town wall so that they could discharge either into the mill leat or the Gyffin stream. They probably served the staff of the king's wardrobe and those under the master of the works, whose offices must have lain just inside the walls.

It is one of no fewer than fifteen examples of twin-towered gateways to be seen at castles and walled towns built in north Wales between 1275 and 1300. Generally these gates consist of a pair of D-shaped towers, like those of the other town gates at Conwy; or they may, as at Rhuddlan, have round towers or, as at Denbigh and Caernarfon Castles, a pair of polygonal towers. The Mill Gate at Conwy, however, differs from all the others in that its towers are not a pair: that on the north is D-shaped, that on the south virtually round. Moreover, unlike the Upper Gate and, so far as can now be seen, the Lower Gate, the upper part of the Mill Gate originally consisted of two well-appointed interconnecting rooms, each of them provided with a full-dress hooded fireplace and each occupying the main floor of one of the towers; the back of the gate at this level was of timber-framed construction, and one must presume that connected to it there was originally another building which contained the stair by which these upper rooms would normally be reached. From the northern room and from the south-west corner of the southern room doors lead on to the top of the town wall.

The stretch of wall to the west, between the Mill Gate and Tower 18, is unlike any other stretch, not merely of the Conwy wall, but also, it is believed, of any other surviving medieval town wall in Europe. For here, symmetrically spaced out between the two towers, are the remains of no fewer than twelve little privies, some still with the grooves for their wooden fronts and seats, projecting from the wall-top so as formerly to have discharged, it must be presumed, either into the mill leat or into a Gyffin stream whose course may once have run closer to the walls than it does today. Nowhere else, except in the reredorters of some of the great monastic houses, is there left to us so extensive and remarkable an example of a multiple medieval sanitary arrangement, primitive in form yet startlingly modern in the repetitiveness of its disposition.

What is the explanation of so elaborate and extraordinary a provision, for the special construction of which, outside the ordinary course of their contract (*pro xij cameris forinescis de opere extra cursum*), the masons were paid £15 in 1286?

A clue to the answer is given by the fact that in the building accounts the item just quoted is found sandwiched immediately between, on the one hand, payments for masonry work described as being on the 'two towers of the Mill Gate' and, on the other, payments for work described as being on the 'towers of the king's wardrobe'. A reference a little further on in the same accounts to other work on the Mill Gate 'and on the Round Tower, namely the tower of the wardrobe of the king's hall' must certainly mean, when read in conjunction with the items quoted previously, that the tower referred to is in fact the round south tower of the Mill Gate, which is thus identified as being one of the towers of the king's wardrobe. These references connecting the king's wardrobe with the vicinity of the Mill Gate are of the greatest interest, and once they are understood it is not difficult to explain the unusual character of the adjacent stretch of the town wall.

The 'wardrobe of the king's hall' or, as the scribe could perhaps have phrased it more intelligibly, the hall of the king's wardrobe, was the name for the building in which the great staff of this department of state lived and worked. It was of timber construction, erected by the king's master carpenter, Henry of

Oxford. Its importance in the administrative organization is reflected in the fact that it was completed within three months of the arrival of the English at Conwy — that is, by June 1283 — by which time the clerks of the wardrobe had already moved into it from nearby temporary accommodation hurriedly put up for them in March. Probably there was physical connection between the wardrobe hall and the timbered back of the Mill Gate, and it is more than likely that the suite on the upper floor of the gate, which after 1312 we find assigned to the chamberlain of north Wales, was at first occupied by the controller of the wardrobe.

There is also evidence to suggest that somewhere nearby, probably between the Mill Gate and the castle on the ground now occupied by the car park, there was, at least from 1286 to 1296, the office of the 'Master of the King's Works in Wales', the number of whose staff one can only assume to have been commensurate with the scale of the great buildings for whose planning and erection he was the officer primarily responsible. There is little doubt that

The King's Wardrobe

By the late thirteenth century, the king's wardrobe — originally simply a place where the royal robes and jewels were kept — had become practically synonymous with the king's private secretariat. In effect, it was becoming, like the chancery and the exchequer, a department of state, its operations touching every branch of administration and finance and conducted from wherever the sovereign might be. During King Edward's Welsh war of 1282–83, and for at least the earlier years of the immense castle-building programme to which in north

Wales that war gave rise, the wardrobe was the department through which war and works alike were principally administered. From 1283 onwards a wardrobe in this sense, and for this very purpose, was located here at Conwy. It was staffed by a body of royal clerks, headed by the keeper or treasurer of the wardrobe and his deputy, the controller. The latter was in effect the secretary of the king's household, and it was he who kept the king's privy seal and supervised the preparation of the immense body of documents issued under its authority.

By the late thirteenth century, the wardrobe was virtually the king's private secretariat. This manuscript records the keeper of the wardrobe's miscellaneous expenses account for Conwy in 1283–84 (Public Record Office E 101/351/9).

There is a superb panorama of the castle and town walls to be gained from the slopes of Benarth Hill across the valley of the Gyffin.

it was for the convenience of these two groups of staff, those under the controller of the wardrobe and those under the master of the works, on whose efficient functioning the whole English policy in north Wales ultimately hinged, that the elaboration of the wall-top west of the Mill Gate was executed.

There are many references in the fourteenth- and fifteenth-century Chamberlains' Accounts to the maintenance of the Mill Gate and its adjacent buildings. In 1312, for example, we read of repairs to 'the houses of the tower which is called *La Mullegate*, assigned for the lodging (*hospicium*) of the Chamberlain'. In 1396 there are payments 'for making a partition in the exchequer of Conway and another in the gate called *le Muleyat*, and for repairing the windows, partitions, roof and other defects in the chamber over *le Muleat*'.

Somewhere in the same quarter of the town there was another official residence, that assigned to the justiciar. In the earliest reference (1286) it appears as 'the hall of the lord Otto', namely Otto de Grandison (d. 1328), the first justiciar appointed after the settlement of 1284. Later accounts show that its buildings included a hall, chambers, kitchen and stable lying within a stone-walled enclosure. It is clear from the records that the justiciar's hall was separate both from Llywelyn's Hall and from the chamberlain's quarters at the Mill Gate. In 1401 a band of Welsh rebels associated with Owain Glyn Dŵr obtained control of the castle by treachery and proceeded to burn all the houses in the town 'together with the bridge at the Upper Gate, the Exchequer [Mill] Gate, and the lodgings of the justiciar and the Chamberlain', doing damage estimated at £5,000.

The Glyn Dŵr rebellion in Wales was relaunched in April 1401 when Conwy was taken in a daredevil raid. It was held by the rebels for several months, with the damage costs later estimated at £5,000. Glyn Dŵr's arms appear on this harness decoration found at Harlech Castle (© National Museums & Galleries of Wales).

They also made off with all the records preserved in the exchequer, including the detailed accounts of works on the castle (*les parcelles des costages pour le reparacion de Chasteill de Conewey*), an incalculable loss for which, if we are to believe the record, damages were assessed even in the money of those days at £10,000. For at least 130 years after this disaster the accounts make no further mention of the Mill Gate, and it is doubtful whether its timbered upper portion was ever rebuilt.

Four stretches of wall and three intervening towers (19, 20 and 21) link the Mill Gate to the castle. They are well seen, as indeed is the whole course eastwards from Tower 13, from the slopes of Benarth Hill across the valley. Both Towers 19 and 20 look somewhat squat through the loss of their battlements, an effect accentuated all along this part

of the wall through the building up of the railway embankment at its foot. Between the Mill Gate and the castle the wall runs alongside the public car park, and its inward face is accessible to view all the way from the gate to where it approaches the castle rock. The wall-walk of this section is also accessible from the north tower in the Mill Gate.

At the far end, the wall is carried down to the full depth of the ditch which here formerly isolated the castle from the town, and which today serves as a cutting for the Llanrwst Road. The wall strides across the gap, the road passing through a nineteenth-century arch below. As on the north side, the wall-walk terminates before the castle is reached, and only a narrow link wall, along which no enemy could approach, is allowed to make contact with the southern tower of the castle barbican.

A view of the castle and the Conwy estuary from the south, with Robert Stephenson's imposing tubular railway bridge of 1848.

Further Reading

A. H. Dodd, *A History of Caernarvonshire 1284–1900* (Caernarfon 1968).

J. Goronwy Edwards, 'Edward I's Castle-Building in Wales', *Proceedings of the British Academy*, 32 (1946), 15–81.

W. J. Hemp, 'Conwy Castle', *Archaeologia Cambrensis*, 96 (1941), 163–74.

H. Harold Hughes, 'The Edwardian Castle and Town Defences at Conwy', *Archaeologia Cambrensis*, 93 (1938), 75–92, 212–25.

J. E. Morris, *The Welsh Wars of Edward I* (Oxford 1901); reprinted (Stroud 1997).

E. Neaverson, *Mediaeval Castles in North Wales: A Study of Sites, Water Supply and Building Stones* (Liverpool and London 1947).

J. R. Phillips, *Memoirs of the Civil War in Wales and the Marches, 1642–1649*, 2 vols. (London 1874).

Michael Prestwich, *Edward I* (London 1988); new edition (New York and London 1997).

Royal Commission on Ancient and Historical Monuments in Wales and Monmouthshire, *An Inventory of the Ancient Monuments in Caernarvonshire, I: East* (London 1956), 46–57.

A. J. Taylor, 'The Walls of Conwy', *Archaeologia Cambrensis*, 119 (1970), 1–9.

A. J. Taylor, 'Castle-Building in Thirteenth-Century Wales and Savoy', *Proceedings of the British Academy*, 63 (1977), 265–92.

A. J. Taylor, 'The Conwy Particulars Accounts for Nov. 1285–Sept. 1286', *Bulletin of the Board of Celtic Studies*, 30 (1982–83), 134–43.

Arnold Taylor, *Four Great Castles* (Newtown 1983).

Arnold Taylor, 'The Dismantling of Conwy Castle', *Transactions of the Ancient Monuments Society*, 29 (1985), 81–9.

Arnold Taylor, *The Welsh Castles of Edward I* (London 1986).

A. J. Taylor, 'The Town and Castle of Conwy: Preservation and Interpretation', *Antiquaries Journal*, 75 (1995), 339–63.

Sidney Toy, 'The Town and Castle of Conway', *Archaeologia*, 86 (1936), 163–93.

R. Williams, *The History and Antiquities of the Town of Aberconwy and its Neighbourhood* (Denbigh 1835).

K. Williams-Jones, 'The Taking of Conwy Castle, 1401', *Transactions of the Caernarvonshire Historical Society*, 39 (1978), 7–43.